LET'S TALK ABOUT THIS

50 THINGS YOU NEED TO KNOW ABOUT STARTING AND MANAGING A SMALL BUSINESS

BOB DAHMS
MBA, CPA, CMA

LET'S TALK ABOUT THIS
50 Things You Need to Know About
Starting and Managing a Small Business

Copyright © 2023 Bob Dahms

To request permissions, contact the publisher at
publishing@villagebooks.com

Paperback: 9780578986142
Library of Congress Number: 2021918220

First paperback edition 2023.

Edited by Christina Nichols
Copyedited by Jessica Mayfield
Cover by BookHouse
Layout by Jill Flores
Produced by Village Books Publishing Department

Printed in the USA by Village Books.

Chuckanut Editions
1200 11th Street
Bellingham, WA 98226

villagebooks.com/village-books-chuckanut-editions

CHUCKANUT
EDITIONS

ACKNOWLEDGEMENTS

My thanks go to Christina Nichols for working through the first draft with many suggestions.

Extra thanks go to Christy Dahms, my wife, for her thorough work on the draft.

And what made it fly was the publishing team of Chloe and Chelanne at Village Books, in Bellingham, Washington.

CONTENTS

Stage Three: **GROWTH** 77

Stage Four: **MATURITY** 111

INTRODUCTION

Starting and managing a small business is quite involved. It is a major step in your career and your life. As a SCORE business counselor working on a one-on-one basis, I **saw the need** for business information to be shared through a greater platform. Over the course of three years, I wrote 115 weekly columns in the Business section of the *Bellingham Herald* in Bellingham, Washington. The response from the community regarding the column, "Let's Talk About This", was so positive, but again, I saw the need for the next step, and for a more permanent reference to provide to readers. Hence, this book was born.

It is very important in business to **see the need**. Filling the need might take different roads as your business develops and your audience grows. Be aware along the way that the need is still there, and make sure you are growing with it. Many things you do in the early stages can have great impact on your future success. Here are some tips:

- First, **offer a product or service that meets a "felt need."** Research this thoroughly.

- Develop a **written business plan** to guide you through the startup process and keep you working on your main goals.

- **Get a mentor.** Contact and work with SCORE (*score.org*) on your startup's progress. It's free and confidential.

- **Manage your cash effectively.** Your business may not be profitable for several months or perhaps longer, so have a cash reserve on hand.

- There are major challenges involved with **hiring your first employee**. If you're unsure about this, get help from an accounting or payroll preparation firm so you know what you're getting into.

- **Build your brand.** Develop some messages and graphics that you will use to present yourself to the world.

- **Keep your focus.** Many daily happenings will need your immediate attention.

  Don't be diverted by the trivial.

- As you grow, **continuously seek to innovate and adapt** your business conditions as the market changes.

- **Always be thinking ahead** as to what problems and opportunities might arise.

This book gives you a great many facts, suggestions, resources, and instructions. Use this book as a guide and a reference – the path to running a small business is not always linear, so neither is this book! I've separated the chapters into themes and in the back you will find a compiled list of resources that are mentioned throughout.

I hope you will use it thoroughly and enjoy the results, as I have.

STAGE ONE:
PRE-STARTUP

This stage is critically important. Give it its due: you'll be glad you did. Take a moment to make a list of your strong knowledge areas, abilities, and skill sets. Also make note of any areas where you will need help. Set an up-front limit on how much you will spend at this stage to make the "go/no-go" decision.

Introductory Thoughts

- A very important product of this stage is the name for your business. Research this carefully.

- Prepare your written business plan. Include key performance indicators (KPIs). Google "free business plan template" for help with this step.

- Form your business entity (LLC or corporation).

- Make any arrangements for a business location, if appropriate.

- Open a business bank account. Begin your cash flow planning.

- It will seem as if there are too many alternatives for everything. Narrow down your choices and move ahead.

- For a moment, think ahead about your exit strategy and when that will be.

- Set up your outside advisory board. This should include help with accounting, legal, banking, and insurance matters. Also, finding someone with experience in your business is extremely helpful.

- For free and confidential business advice, check in with SCORE (*score.org*), a large network of volunteer, expert business mentors for small businesses. Another great resource is Small Business Development Center (*americassbdc.org*). Go to their website and enter your zip code for local and easy access.

- Join any relevant professional or trade associations.

- Expect to spend a great deal of your time on your business.

1 SOME THOUGHTS TO GET YOU STARTED

QUESTION:
I'm confident that my startup business idea is workable, but I'm a little weak on the actual business essentials. What are some basic must-knows to get off the ground?

ANSWER:
This is a common question from new entrepreneurs. It's time to set out the Top 10 Business Essentials. These concepts and ideas may be new to you.

Let's talk about this.

1. **Be conscious of your branding.** You'll hear businesspeople talk about their hot idea, new customer, or potential super location. But remember that the most important component of your new business is YOU. Especially when you first start out into the business world, you **are** your branding. Make sure you're always ready to present yourself professionally and on an instant's notice.

   If you don't already have attractive business cards, local printshops have starter packages at a modest cost. If you're just testing a business idea, you can get 100 good-quality cards for under $20 at several online sites (Google "100 business cards") or go to *avery.com* for free software to print your own and print them on special cardstock (like Avery 8371). You can make as few as ten cards at a time; just snap them apart, and you're good to go.

2. **You need several exciting versions of your elevator speech.** Of course this is a metaphor. To refresh, your elevator speech is your response to an imaginary question asked of you by someone getting

on an elevator with you. They might say, "You look familiar. Do I know you?" Don't do the deer-in-the-headlights act. Instead, you have around fifteen seconds to jump into your smooth elevator speech and tell them:

- Who you are

- What you do

- Why they need you

- How they can reach you

Rehearse and perfect your mini-introduction.

If you're having trouble crafting your elevator speech, here's a tip: try working through these three steps. First, practice your delivery to a child, so you keep it simple. Second, practice your delivery to your mother so you're sure it's ethical. Third, practice your delivery to an established businessperson. Of course, this last version becomes your "real" speech. Other versions are OK too, as appropriate. For example: a humorous version would be suitable at a chamber of commerce after-hours social event.

3. **Subscribe to all of the relevant trade magazines.** Nearly every business has several dedicated magazines. They're usually free because trade magazines make most of their income by offering your eyeballs to their advertisers. The higher their readership, the more ad revenue they can generate.

   You'll learn the trade jargon and the latest news and trends in your field. You can note important companies, people, products, and events. As soon as it makes financial sense, visit the largest trade show you can justify. If your business is small, you may need to budget ahead for travel expenses. Visit the Trade Shows News Network website (*tsnn.com*) for a searchable database of trade shows in every imaginable field of business.

4. **Unify the design and appearance of all your company's visuals.** This includes your logo, signage, business cards, web presence, letterhead, uniforms, vehicles, etc. Use the same font, same layout, and same colors on anything that identifies your brand to your

target market. Larger firms have entire graphics departments to do this. If your visuals seem disorganized and lightweight, your company will too.

It's fairly common to see a young business with incongruent and unappealing visuals. This is a problem that is pretty easy, and not too expensive, to correct. Ask a businessperson whom you admire for some informal advice. When you're ready, find an intern in graphic design to help you out in return for college credit.

5. **Set up your accounting properly.** Get help if this isn't your forte. Consider this: if you blunder through setting up your books, you'll actually pay for it, in time or money, three times! The first is your time and pain to set it up incorrectly. The second is paying to have someone undo what you did. And the third is paying to have it redone properly.

   Go to the Internal Revenue Service website (*irs.gov*) and download a Schedule C and a Publication 583. The latter has very good information, in straight talk, about the purpose of your books and how to set them up. Also consider using software like QuickBooks. If this isn't for you, there are many local bookkeeping services; ask around.

   When you have employees, definitely get help unless (1) you feel very confident processing payroll by yourself, and (2) there is no other, more valuable use of your time.

6. **Take advantage of state agencies' free training seminars and websites.** Start with the department of revenue because most every business will need to register with and report to them.

   If you have employees or are looking at hiring, be sure to get acquainted with your state departments of labor and employment security. Many have training opportunities. Some states also offer a safety assessment of your workplace at no cost.

7. **Use local sources of help.** Schedule a SCORE counseling session. Start at *score.org*. Enter your zipcode and click on "Match me by zip code". Talk with an experienced businessperson about your idea, problem, or question. It's free, informal, and confidential.

Check with your local community and technical colleges for small business classes and training seminars.

Be aware of the numerous other local sources of business help. It's worth your time to look into how these organizations can help you and your business. Examples:

- Local chamber of commerce
- Local Small Business Development Center
- Your city's economic development department

8. **Build a resource library, and share it with others.** These can be physical books, e-books, websites you've bookmarked, business blogs, or newspaper and magazine articles. Book suggestions:

   - *Small Time Operator* by Bernard B. Kamoroff C.P.A.
   - *The Small Business Bible* by Steven D. Strauss
   - *Why We Buy* by Paco Underhill
   - *Complete Idiot's Guide* business books (such as *Business Law* and *Business Management*) and the *For Dummies* series (such as *Branding for Dummies* and *Starting a Business for Dummies*) are generally very good.
   - For legal matters, NOLO (*nolo.com*) has high-quality books and also a strong website.

   Both the Small Business Administration (SBA, at *sba.gov*) and SCORE (*score.org*) websites are loaded with valuable content. Here are a few other sites with lots of good material:

   - National Federation of Independent Businesses (*nfib.com*)
   - Business Know-How (*businessknowhow.com*)
   - Palo Alto Software (*paloalto.com*)
   - IRS small business/self-employed site (*irs.gov/businesses/small-businesses-self-employed*)

9. **Revisit your business plan monthly.** These are the benchmarks for measuring how your business is doing against your established goals. A typical young business should do a prompt monthly

financial analysis (comparing actual results with the budgeted projections) during the first several years. This monthly feedback is essential for making good decisions. Be especially watchful of your cash flow. If you're chronically out of cash, pretty soon you're out of business.

Your business plan is a living document. It's OK to revise it as needed. For example, if you had a bad sales month last March, it might be appropriate to consider revising next March's sales forecast downward. **But never** retroactively lower your financial objectives just so you can say you met them.

10. **Be optimistic but also realistic.** Dave Ramsey, the national TV and radio financial guru, once urged an owner of a startup to bear in mind three important facts:

> **No. 1:** It will cost twice as much as you think it will.
>
> **No. 2:** It will take twice as long as you think it will.
>
> **No. 3:** You think you'll be the exception to the first two — but you won't.

Hopefully these startup thoughts will give you some ideas for getting your business going on solid footing. There's plenty of help available; seek it out.

2 WHAT'S IN A (BUSINESS) NAME?

QUESTION:
I'm thinking about some possible names for my new business. Is this a big deal or not? I guess I could change it if I misfire the first time. What do I need to know about naming my new business?

ANSWER:
Well, let me be frank with you here. I think you should step back and get more serious about your business and its name. Realize that you are working on one of the most important steps in starting your business. Consider this: For the first several months your business is in operation, your name will be all that the public — your prospective customers — will see, hear, or have much knowledge of.

Let's talk about this.

We'll look at some tips for naming a business, as well as some traps to avoid. But first off, an important note: most of what follows also applies for an existing business looking at naming a new product or service that it might offer. Large companies are experts at this. Examples: McDonald's McRib Meal, Kellogg's Pringles, and Toyota's Lexus brand. These are all coined (made-up) names not in the dictionary. You too can give a proprietary name to your business or product and trademark it.

Here are some basics about naming a business. It's important that you get this right the first time. Having to later rename and rebrand a business is very disruptive; it's confusing to your customers and clients and also expensive.

Get some outside help. If you're drawing a blank, you might find a jump-start at an online business name generator site. Here are three: *biznamewiz.com, namefind.com,* and *panabee.com.* Look for simple, catchy names that are descriptive and memorable. Also, keep a thesaurus handy to look up synonyms and related ideas.

Using your own personal name is easy and tempting but it has some real drawbacks. It can seriously narrow the field of people who would be interested in eventually buying your business. A better idea is to gather some creative friends, host a party, and brainstorm some names that relate to what you do.

Consider whether a geographical name reference fits. These can be helpful initially but might be a real problem later on. For a small and local business, a name like Whatcom Auto Repair or Mt. Baker Salon is probably OK, but if you have growth aspirations, it could be a serious liability. And what if Cornwall Avenue Books moves to Meridian Street?

Make sure it sounds good. A person who hears your business name should be able to write it down. This is called the "radio test" because it originated back when marketing people tested ads on a small radio across the room. When you have focused down to a handful of names, it's easy to get a small group of people together and test this. Just read the list and have them write the names down. See how they did in hearing them correctly. If the name is not understandable or has to be spelled out, dump it.

Avoid using just initials. Some people think that the initialed names of companies like IBM, 3M, KFC, and HP contributed to their success. But the fact is that all of these companies, and many others with names like theirs, actually started out and grew successfully for decades with long, spelled-out names.

Top-of-alphabet names like AAA Construction and Aardvark Hair Salon don't work now. That gimmick only worked for phone books.

Include some catchy value or content. This will help make the name memorable. One technique is to use alliteration, like "Transmission Tune-ups." Or, you can suggest value, like "Maid for You" or "Lean Cuisine." In marketing speak, this is called "stickiness."

Visualize your logo. Think about how your business name could work into an attractive logo. Here's where initials might come into play: consider using the formula of consonant-vowel-consonant for the first letters of the words constituting the name. For example, Northwest Engineering Team might be able to build "NET" into a good logo.

Be website-ready. Every business should have multiple domain and social networking names that match.

Test out your ideas. Once you have your short list together, write the names on separate cards. Then, ask several people to go through the cards and rank them from most to least favored. Keep track of their responses. Also, be sure to Google each name to avoid cultural surprises. Example: the Chevrolet Nova in Spanish, "No va" means "it won't go".

Check on trademarking. As a last step in your name selection process, verify that you can trademark your name with the U.S. Patent and Trademark Office (*uspto.gov*). Also check out *trademarkia.com*.

Register with the state. If you expect to form an LLC or a corporation, be sure to check with your Secretary of State and register the name before you file any other applications.

Name on!

3 | AM I READY, OR NOT?

QUESTION:

I have an idea to start a new business, but I'm just not sure I'm ready to act on it. Something is holding me back. Is this just normal jitters about taking the leap? Or is there something wrong with my business idea — or with me?

ANSWER:

Well, you may be right to question your readiness. There are very common reasons for your hesitation, which we'll look at in some detail.

Let's talk about this.

First off, a very important concept: all of the supportive folks around you, like your friends and relatives, are probably acting as your cheerleading section. They are rooting you on with the best of intentions — but they may have little or no relevant business experience or training. Here's the big problem; that's not really the type of advice you need right now.

Sure, it's important to have support and encouragement. Right now, what you need even more is some pushback. You need to talk with a knowledgeable businessperson who asks questions and challenges some of your assumptions. It's a bit like when a true friend tells you in a social setting that you have spinach in your teeth. The intention here is to focus in on possible trouble spots for your business. If your plan has an obvious fatal flaw, wouldn't you want to know about it?

Your startup has two major areas of concern. The first is your business model itself. This explains exactly how you will offer value (something people will pay for) to your prospective customers and clients. The second concern is about you — your personal knowledge, abilities, and managerial skill sets.

Here are some examples of questions about your business model:

- Did you determine the potential market for your products and services? Do they meet an existing "felt need"?

- Exactly what is unique about your product or service? If it's already offered, why will yours be better and capture a market share? If it's brand new, how will you generate awareness?

- Do you have a written business plan? If not, you need to get to work on this, pronto. For help, go to *score.org/startup-resources* and see what looks suitable and helpful.

- Have you laid out a strong online presence and strategy?

- How long will it take for the business to have positive cash flow?

And here are some questions about you:

- What experience in any similar business field do you have? This could be as an employee or even a college intern.

- Have you operated any kind of business before? What level of business management skills do you have?

- Do you realize that your technical skills are completely different from your business skills?

- Are you able to wear all of the hats in the early stages of your business? Think of yourself as the CEO — the Chief Everything Officer.

- Can you make decisions when not all the information is in hand? Running a business requires making judgment calls while also weighing the risk of making a wrong decision.

- What backup financial reserves do you have? Your business may not have positive cash flow as quickly as you expect it to. Do you have personal or family resources, or borrowing power, to cover it?

- Are you comfortable negotiating? Being in business is a constant process of dealmaking. This includes vendors, suppliers, clients, customers, employees — it never stops.

- Can you handle confrontation? As the owner, you will have to deal with the occasional angry client, customer, or naysayer. You need to have skills to diffuse and resolve these situations.

- How is your personal energy level? Starting a business has been compared to having a newborn baby. It's a 24/7 job.

- Can you delegate? If not, you will have trouble growing.

- Where do you want to be in five years? Put some thought into this.

So here's the bottom line: you may or may not be ready to start your business right now. That's important to know because a major cause of business failure is launching unprepared.

Nationally known business author Carol Roth has excellent self-assessment information. Go to *carolroth.com* and click on "Community" from the menu tab. You'll get a real eyeful of frank business thought. Choose a few. And remember that you can get free, confidential, in-person advice at any stage of your business by contacting SCORE (*score.org*) or your local Small Business Development Center.

4 I'LL NEED FINANCING

QUESTION:

I'm starting a business but I'm brand new with no track record. So, what's the deal for me? Is a bank loan out of my reach?

ANSWER:

Getting conventional bank financing for a startup business is a challenge. This situation is very different from (and considerably more difficult than) an existing business wanting to expand. Realize that you are in a pretty weak bargaining position. You'll need to be very creative in finding alternative financing sources. However, there are several ways to get started.

Let's talk about this.

First off, be aware that several commonly mentioned funding sources are not realistic for the vast majority of startup or early-stage businesses. These include venture capital sources, formal crowdfunding, angel investor groups, and hard money lenders.

We'll look at sixteen ways to finance a business startup. These don't all apply to every business; you will need to be opportunistic. We'll look at some funding possibilities, noting the downsides associated with each. Remember, every business decision is a tradeoff of plusses and minuses. You're probably eager to get the business up and going but don't allow that eagerness to rush you into a risky or unsuitable financial arrangement.

Next, you should get a handle on where you are financially right now. The best way to do this is to step back and look at your personal financial statement. Of most interest is the balance sheet, which is basically a listing of your financial assets and liabilities. For a blank form, go to any bank, or go visit *sba.gov* and enter "Form 413" in the search box. Spend a while filling in estimates of the values of all your assets and any amounts you owe.

With your financial data in hand, let's look at some common forms of business startup financing.

Invest personal equity. Of course, the most desirable source of startup capital is your own money. If you have savings or other similarly liquid funds, you're literally in business. It doesn't have to be big money if you're starting out small. On the downside, it's obvious that if your business fails, the money is gone.

Use the Three Fs. This is a bit of a joke in the business finance community; it stands for "family, friends, and fools." A great many business startups get funding from family members. This is fine, but be sure you have a written agreement (say, a promissory note with repayment terms and an interest rate) so everyone agrees about whether it's a loan, a gift, or a purchase of part of the company. This is especially important with friends or "fools" where blood is not so thick. The downside is that you risk damaging a personal relationship if things go south.

Sell some assets. You may find that you have some items you could sell, like a coin collection or a classic car. This frees up cash to put into the business. Of course, you will no longer have the asset.

Use credit cards. A good way: buy resale merchandise and supplies with the ability to pay later. This lessens your need to put in big money up front. A bad way: take large cash advances. You'll pay a high interest rate, 20 percent or more.

Dip into a retirement plan, like an IRA. It seems to be a ready source of cash, but be very careful. Under common circumstances, you'll get hit with income taxes and a hefty penalty. Get advice before you do this.

Ask someone to cosign for a loan. This may be a possibility if you have a supporter with good credit who is willing to step up. Of course, the cosigner becomes personally liable if you default and can't repay.

Use a home equity loan. If you or a backer has home equity, this may sound like a good idea. Interest rates on home equity loans are very low because the lender is a secured creditor. But here's the problem: the backer is securing your loan with his or her personal home. If your business fails, they are on the hook to repay the loan.

Borrow against a solid asset. Something that you own, but can't part with, might be good collateral for a bank loan. A paid-for RV or some stock certificates might yield substantial cash. The longer lived the asset, the lower the loan payments will be.

Take in a partner. The partnership agreement should spell out exactly what role the partner has in the business, from a passive investor (silent partner) to full, active involvement. It's common for the agreement to allow you to buy out the partner's interest at a future time at agreed-upon terms.

Lease some needed equipment. While it's more expensive in the long run than buying, leasing saves precious up-front cash. This is most appropriate when you know you will need a particular vehicle or machine for several years. Read the lease agreement carefully; it could have terms and conditions you may want to negotiate.

Draw cash from a life insurance policy. This is easy to do. The cash value of a term policy will be much less than the face value. Of course the drawback is that the death benefit decreases.

Try a peer-to-peer (P2P) online microlending site. Sites like *prosper.com* and *lendingclub.com* offer to match up small borrowers and lenders. As with anything else on the internet, be careful. Several sites that appear to offer independent reviews of P2P lenders are actually affiliated with them.

Manage your cash flow. One of the best ways to reduce your need to borrow is to manage your cash very effectively. Your new mantra is "Make one dollar do the work of three." Here are some examples of sharp cash management:

- Ask a landlord for low rent in initial months, ramping up after that.
- Offer good clients a discount for paying for services promptly.
- Negotiate delayed payment terms with vendors.

- Ride herd on expenses. Depending on your margins, $1 spent may negate $5 to $10 in sales.
- If you hold an inventory, keep it to a minimum and turn it quickly.

Look into set-asides. Many governmental units at both federal and state levels require that some percentage of purchases go to small or minority-owned businesses. Google "small business set-asides," and see what you might be able to go for. There's some hassle involved, but it's a good way to get your foot in the door for government contracts.

Keep your day job. Some people can start up their business while still working, perhaps cutting back to half-time. But be aware that cutting your hours announces to your employer that you're a "short-timer." You may also give up substantial benefits like medical insurance.

And last, don't totally rule out a local bank loan. One strategy: get your credit report and FICO score at *annualcreditreport.com*. Credit reports are free and a FICO score is around $10. Look it over for errors and then go to the bank you use the most and ask to talk with a banker about your credit and your business idea. This may allow you to strike up a relationship for the future.

5 WHAT DO I NEED TO KNOW ABOUT BUSINESS PLANS?

QUESTION:
I'm working on writing my business plan and I'm confused by the conflicting information about what to include. Four pages, or thirty? Just the big picture, or heavy on the details? Can you help me?

ANSWER:
Yes, it is confusing, and I'll tell you why. The short answer is: It depends on the purpose of your plan and your intended audience.

Let's talk about this.

If your business is on the small side, you aren't seeking any financing, and the business plan is primarily for your own use, then the four-pager is probably just fine. The other extreme would be where you're looking for a bank loan or you intend to offer a new or high-tech idea or an untested product. If so, you'll need to do substantially more work.

Also, realize that business plans are appropriate not just for startups, but for numerous existing businesses and other situations too. Some examples: launching a major new product, opening a new location, convincing a new supplier to give you a large credit line, adding a related but innovative service, or expanding into a new demographic market. Additionally, a growing company might prepare a confidential strategic or marketing plan for internal use.

That said, there are some common elements of most basic business plans. Typically, a simple plan will typically contain at least these sections, more or less in this order:

- **Executive summary** — features the highlights of your plan and develops your idea in two pages or less. Warning! It seems goofy but write this first section last, after you've finished the rest of the plan. This is because you'll have a much clearer idea of how your business will work after you've finished the sections discussed below. Be aware that many readers of business plans scan the executive summary and make an instant decision on whether they're going to read any further or throw it on the heap. Put some horsepower into this section.

Then, you'll need to address some internal aspects of the business:

- **Company summary** — gives a brief description of your company and its structure (proprietor, LLC, corporation), ownership, and history.

- **Management summary** — provides background on the management team, their experience, and their key accomplishments.

- **Products or services** — describes these and how they stand out from the competition. A current term for this is your "unique value proposition."

Next, show your research on your target market and how you expect to reach it:

- **Market analysis** — provides a summary of your intended or typical customers, competitive landscape, market size, and expected market growth.

- **Strategy and implementation** — describes how you will generate sales and how you will put your plan into action. This section also establishes milestones and metrics for how you will measure your progress toward your goals.

Last, the numbers need to flow:

- **Financial plan** — contains key financial analysis and projections including balance sheets, sales and expenses, cash flow, and other information, as appropriate. The common standard is Excel spreadsheets. Depending on the nature and purpose of your business plan, this section could be as simple as a few pages. If more complex, this information is better shown in a financial appendix.

A common question is, "Should I have an expert write my business plan for me?" The answer is NO. That would completely defeat the purpose of you writing the plan. The value of the plan is not so much having the finished document in hand as the process you went through to prepare it.

The national SCORE website, *score.org*, has advice, templates, and sample plans. Other ideas: Google "free business plan templates" and see if something you find is a fit for you. The SBA website has hundreds of business plans and lots of helpful ideas — check them out at *sba.gov*. Another excellent source of business plans can be found at *bplans.com/ sample-business-plans*. You can also buy inexpensive software to help you out. The top seller is Business Plan Pro from Palo Alto Software. In doing your research, don't overlook your local public library's reference librarians. They have access to information and databases that you can't get as an individual.

Last thoughts: expect creating your business plan to take the time equivalent to a part-time job. And get help, even if you think you don't need it.

6 LOW-COST BUSINESS STARTUP IDEAS

QUESTION:
I'm familiar with some general points about starting a business with just a little cash. I'm really interested in doing this. What are some specific business ideas that I might look into?

ANSWER:
That's great. You probably have more skill sets than you realize. Some of these may very well be marketable as viable business ideas.

Let's talk about this.

First, take an inventory of your personal strengths. Make a list of your skills, knowledge areas, interests, hobbies, talents, artistic abilities, and so forth. If other people frequently compliment you on how good you are at something, it should definitely be on your list.

Second, look back over your job history and note any specialized training or proficiencies you have. This should include any experience from volunteering.

Third, make a list of any physical assets you own, or have access to, that may be usable in a business.

And last, let's review six basic rules for any business startup:

1. Rule number one is: it's all about cash flow. If you mismanage this, your business is dead. Get help the minute you realize you need it.

2. Prepare a written business plan with appropriate level of detail.

3. Find a mentor or advisor willing to work with you.

4. Set up a basic home office and treat it as a place of business.

5. Make sure you have all the needed licenses and registrations.

6. Set up your books properly from the start, and keep business and personal money separate.

Just as a discussion starter, below are twelve areas where a person could get a business off the ground with little cash up front. Within each area, I've listed a few examples but use your imagination too. If one of these works for you, that's the objective.

Personal services are always in demand. If you have talents along these lines, get some business cards printed (try *gotprint.com*, under $10) and go test the market.

- Hair care, nails, cosmetics
- Physical fitness coaching
- Shopping and errands (gofer) service
- Income tax preparation

Teaching and tutoring have nearly unlimited opportunities.

- Computer skills, internet use
- Musical instrument instruction
- Academic subjects (e.g., math, foreign languages)

Leisure time activities are a fun way to interact with people.

- Hobbies
- Collectibles and antiques
- Stamps and coins
- Dance instruction

Outside home and yard work are perpetual needs, but seasonal.

- Mowing, tree pruning
- Painting
- Window washing

Pet services are big business. The American Pet Products Association says Americans spend over $100 billion a year on their pets. If you like animals, providing these services is fairly easy and low stress.

- Grooming and sitting
- Obedience training and exercising
- Vacation feeding

Caregiving to others is in high need. Entry requirements are fairly low.

- Child care
- Elder care
- Caregiver relief
- Food and meal supervision

Transportation is essential. For those without a car, it's a payable necessity.

- Car ride to a medical appointment
- Driving kids home from school
- Picking up groceries or prescriptions

In-home help is very sellable, especially to two-worker households.

- Laundry and cleaning, meal preparation
- Supervising children
- Bill paying

Online opportunities are limitless.

- Buying/selling goods on Craigslist (*craigslist.org*)
- Selling hand crafted items on Etsy (*etsy.com*)
- Language translation
- Website design and maintenance

Cleaning and detailing services. You'll need a pressure washer and some supplies.

- Cars and boats

- Patios, roofs, and decks
- Driveways

Hauling services can be an easy startup if you have a truck or trailer.

- Debris removal, construction site cleanup
- Dump runs
- Furniture pickup/delivery, help with moving

Services for businesses come in many varieties.

- Janitorial services
- Security detail for retailers
- Temporary work (vacation fill-in)

Important final thought: picture yourself meeting someone's "felt need." This means you will offer a solution to a recognized need or problem and quickly add value to someone's life or business. Good luck.

7 TWO ALTERNATIVES TO STARTING A BUSINESS

> **QUESTION:**
> *I'm confident I could run a business but I don't feel skilled or patient enough to start one from scratch. What are the alternatives, and are they a good idea?*
>
> **ANSWER:**
> *Yes, this happens every day. Two major alternatives are (1) buying an existing business, and (2) investing in a franchise.*
>
> *Let's talk about this.*

WOW! Giving birth to a business is a lot of work. There are numerous instances where a person simply doesn't have the time, the organizational skills, or the physical space to pull it off. That might make **buying an existing business** with a track record look pretty good.

First off, as a potential buyer, recognize that selling a business is a very emotional decision. People want to sell for a whole variety of personal reasons. Sometimes the reason makes financial sense for a new owner and sometimes it doesn't. For many small businesses, common reasons to sell are retirement, personal or family health issues, burnout, and lack of succession (no one to take over). And of course, there may be no reason given, or a false one.

So frankly, owners rarely sell because things are A-OK and they want to sell a profitable business at a high price. More often, they want to sell to get out from under the business. This is a pessimistic but realistic view.

For you as a possible buyer, that's not all bad, but it means you have to do a very thorough analysis of whatever buying opportunities you might find. Your financial analysis for a very small business may be based on limited financial information, perhaps just tax returns and what you can observe. A bit larger business should produce some monthly financial statements (balance sheet and income statement), which will likely be done on QuickBooks or a similar program and will probably be internally prepared. A larger business should have an appropriate level of outside accounting involvement in the financials.

Larger cities have business brokerages, and some real estate firms do business listings as a sideline. Your best bet is to get the word out that you're looking to buy. Commercial bankers would be a good starting point. Follow the local print media for business opportunity ads; check Craigslist.

There are two very sticky areas where you will definitely need professional advice. First, should you buy the business entity or just selected assets? If you buy the entity, you're getting it all: equipment, inventory, accounts receivable — but also liabilities, both known and unknown. If you buy specific assets, you can pick and choose. For example, it's fairly common for the seller to keep the accounts receivable. If you buy an asset that has debt against it, like equipment, it's customary for you to assume the debt.

Second is the valuation issue. This is a huge concern because unlike real estate, businesses don't have directly comparable sales to help establish a price. Nearly every situation is unique, and the older rule of thumb formulas based on gross sales are seldom used now. The company's balance sheet must be examined closely. Is the inventory "clean"? Are the accounts receivable collectable? Is the equipment well maintained?

As to the income statement or tax return, the bottom line is just the starting point for analysis. An experienced business valuation accountant will make numerous adjustments to the net income line. Some will be additions (e.g., add back the depreciation expense); others will be deductions (e.g.. if owner took less than a market salary). The product of this analysis is an amount called owner's discretionary cash flow, which is a very helpful factor in price negotiations.

By the way, during this process you may be told by someone on the seller's side that there is substantial additional off-books or cash income, and that the business has been paying lots of personal expenses. Ignore this.

The final agreed price will also reflect other factors such as if the seller is providing financing, the presence of intangibles like goodwill or intellectual property, a favorable lease, or if the business has long-term sales contracts with strong customers.

Clearly, buying an existing business is one alternative to starting up from scratch. Let's talk about the other common alternative: **investing in a franchise**. Franchise businesses have a much higher success rate than general business startups — but there are tradeoffs, too.

Basically, a franchise is a contractual agreement and relationship between an owner of intellectual property (like patents, trademarks, logos, or service marks) and another party seeking to use that identification in a business. A great many businesses that you see every day are franchises. Common examples include many auto dealerships, real estate companies, fast food outlets, and income tax preparation services. The franchise concept dates back to the late 1800s.

First, I suggest that you think of a franchise startup as more like renting a business. Some people are not comfortable with this idea. Granted, you are in business for yourself, but not with the freedom to "do it my way." If you have a high need for control, it's probably not for you.

That said, here are some of the major pros and cons. Operating a franchise can be like having a supportive partner who already knows the ropes. As a franchise owner, you work under a demonstrated and successful business model. You have access to established operating and marketing strategies. The goods and services are proven. But franchise ownership isn't just an easy shortcut to success. As with any other kind of small business, you still have to commit money, time, and effort to meet both the franchisor's requirements and your own goals. There will be a significant up-front fee and ongoing royalties.

Here's how it works. In the simplest and most basic form of franchising, the franchisee (that's you) buys the rights to use specified names or trademarks for an agreed period of time. This is called a "product or trade name franchise." Scaling up to a more complex form, which is called "business format franchising," there is a much broader and ongoing relationship between the two parties. For example, the franchisor may provide a full range of services, such as help with site selection, product training, and marketing materials. They may supply the actual product for sale (e.g., for car dealers) or some components of the product, or materials to manufacture it (e.g., for fast food outlets). They will certainly regulate the franchisee's compliance with the franchise agreement very closely. As you might guess, penalties for violating that agreement are pretty harsh.

Be aware that many franchisors retain some locations or even large prime geographic areas for themselves. These locations are often called "company ops." This can be a good thing because the franchisor has the motivation and ability to try new products and ideas, which it can then roll out to make its franchisees more successful. It's a win-win.

Recently, franchisors have been aggressively courting veterans. These companies have found that vets are accustomed to operating in a structured environment and do especially well as franchisees. If this interests you, Google "veteran franchise opportunities." Also, AARP encourages those over 50 to become franchisees. For more on this, go to *aarp.org/work/small-business*. And *Forbes* and *Entrepreneur* magazines have done good articles on this exact topic — check their websites.

Another great resource is the International Franchise Association. Their website (*franchise.org*) has loads of good information on nearly every aspect of franchising. There is also a searchable database of 1,400 current franchise opportunities. You will be stunned by the amount and variety of what is available.

Be sure to do your homework before jumping into a franchise deal. A few bad performers can seriously damage it for all, as has happened with Quiznos, Ben and Jerry's, and the UPS Store franchises. For a real eye-opener, Google "franchise horror stories" or go to *unhappyfranchisee.com*.

We need to talk for a moment about a very important item that franchisors are required to supply to prospective franchisees. The Federal Trade Commission, responding to many past abuses, requires every franchisor to provide a franchise disclosure document (FDD) at ten days prior to the signing of the franchise agreement. The FDD, as its name suggests, has a very standardized format. It requires disclosure of all material facts, including any dirty laundry of the franchisor. Some examples include:

- Litigation and bankruptcy history of the franchisor
- Exclusive areas of territory granted
- All fees and expenses
- Required product purchases by franchisee
- Restrictions on other goods and services offered by franchisee

And last, here's a thought about your financing. If you're considering applying for a loan backed by the Small Business Administration, visit the SBA's Franchise Registry at *franchiseregistry.com*. This service lists names of companies whose franchisees enjoy a streamlined review process for SBA loan applications.

8 PROS AND CONS OF PARTNERSHIPS

QUESTION:
The idea of going into business alone scares me. Seems like it would be much easier to share the job with someone else who has complementary talents. Is this true, or am I just looking for the easy way?

ANSWER:
The thought of forming a partnership may be appealing if you're considering launching a small business. But there is way more to consider here.

Let's talk about this.

Unlike solo ventures where all the burdens fall on a single person (that's you), partnerships spread responsibilities. Partners should bring different skills and knowledge to the business. This is very good. For example, one partner may be great with numbers and planning while the other is a whiz at marketing and sales. Combining these elements can open more doors and help the business realize more opportunities more quickly than it could with only one person involved. It can be a win-win situation.

Done properly, a partnership can be really beneficial for all involved. However, partnerships have many potential downsides as well. At worst, conflicts waste time and money. Internal strife erodes focus and strategic direction, causes emotional and financial pain, and can even destroy your business and reputation, says David Gage, a business mediator and partnership expert. Gage, who is author of *The Partnership Charter*, lists seven cautions that would-be and existing partners should consider:

1. If you think you are not partner material, don't take the partner path.

2. Use extreme caution when selecting a partner.

3. If you don't really need a partner, don't get one.

4. If it doesn't feel good before you start, follow your gut and don't do it.

5. Don't be fooled into thinking that legal agreements and documents will keep you out of trouble with one another.

6. If you currently have a partner and it does not feel like a positive working relationship, don't just ignore it. Try to fix things.

7. If there are unanswered questions or vague boundaries and responsibilities with current partners, address these issues while you are still getting along.

These are pretty harsh, but realize that the failure rate for partnerships is much higher than for other forms of business.

A valuable resource for prospective partnerships is *nolo.com*, an excellent site with lots of legal information for consumers and small businesses. Their website has loads of free information specifically about partnerships. Also look at *rocketlawyer.com* for more ideas and customizable documents.

Although a partnership is automatically created when more than one owner starts a business, that's not automatically a good arrangement: it's much too informal and lacks the protections partners are wise to have. You'll certainly need a written partnership agreement. Go to *score.org* and enter "partnership agreement" in the search box. Some essentials of that document:

- Who are the partners, and exactly how will ownership be shared? Is it 50/50 or some other agreed-upon formula?

- How will management duties be decided? Some partnerships rotate the managing partner each year. Clearly lay out each person's roles and responsibilities.

- What are the long-term goals and timeline for the company? Be very clear.

- How will profits and losses be distributed?
- Will it be a limited partnership? This is where the partners have very different roles. Look into this.
- How will disputes be decided? A format in which everyone agrees up front how disagreements will be resolved is a good idea.
- What is the procedure for dealing with the departure or death of a partner?

A partnership is a very flexible and easy form of business ownership, but be aware of the hazards. As always, seek legal and accounting advice before making decisions on this important matter.

9 IS THE LLC ROUTE RIGHT FOR ME?

QUESTION:
I hear that forming a limited liability company (LLC) is one way to structure my new business. Lately it seems like everyone I talk to says that the LLC is the only way to go but I'm uncertain, so what are some pros and cons?

ANSWER:
It's true that many states' laws make it very easy to form an LLC. However, don't just jump into an LLC until you're sure it's the right path for you.

Let's talk about this.

Briefly, here's the deal. You can form an LLC in ten minutes on your Secretary of State's website. Typically, all you need is your desired name (and maybe a couple of alternatives) for your LLC and a credit card for the filing fee. In a few days, you'll get your certificate of formation in the mail — you're official!

Your LLC will need an operating agreement (Google "free LLC operating agreement"). This document spells out the structure and operations of the company. It doesn't need to be filed or recorded with anyone, but take a copy of it to the bank when you set up the LLC accounts. There is often confusion, with good reason, between member-managed and manager-managed LLCs. If you manage the LLC, then it's member-managed.

But just because forming an LLC is simple doesn't mean it meets your particular needs. You should get legal and accounting advice before you do this. Perhaps one of the other common business structures (sole proprietorship, partnership, or corporation) would be a better route for you.

For most businesses, the two biggest **pros** to operating as an LLC are liability issues and income tax matters. There are other considerations as well, but let's deal with these two for now.

First, as to liability, the LLC can be a backstop that shields you from personal liability. If things went haywire and the LLC ended up with debts or lawsuit judgments, your personal assets would enjoy some protection from being grabbed. Remember that you must keep the LLC's financial and other dealings separate from your personal activities or you risk losing the liability protection.

Some business activities have inherent risk. A sole proprietor should look at an LLC (or a corporate) business structure if the business has anything to do with:

- Food products or service
- Children
- Personal services
- Alcohol sales or service
- Vehicles
- Chemicals or hazardous or flammable materials
- Construction or the use of heavy equipment
- Any other activities with an above-average chance of harm to people or property

Talk with your insurance agent about your particular exposures. Some of them can be addressed with a business owner's policy (BOP) package.

Second, as to federal income taxation, your LLC business can choose to be taxed as a pass-through entity. This means that you report your business income directly on your personal tax return. A one-owner LLC does not file a separate tax return.

A common misconception about LLCs goes like this: "I'll get a bank loan as the LLC, and then if I have trouble paying it back, I'm not on the hook." That doesn't happen. In reality, you will have to sign personally for the loan, even if it is in the LLC's name.

Other pros of the LLC business structure are the minimal formalities and reporting requirements when compared to a corporation. There are no traditional board of directors, required annual meetings, or minutes book. The LLC files a one-page annual report with the Secretary of State and pays a modest renewal fee.

On the **con** side, a full-service LLC setup with legal and accounting services could run about $1,500. If you're converting from a proprietorship, the LLC will need all new accounts with the various state and local governmental agencies, a new taxpayer identification number with the IRS, and new bank accounts. You will need to redo all of your printed materials with the new name, and update your website and logo as well.

Now it's time to talk with your advisory board and decide what's best for your particular situation.

10 AM I TOO OLD FOR A BUSINESS STARTUP?

QUESTION:
I'm coming up on the big five-oh birthday. According to AARP, I will then officially become a senior citizen. Is it too late for me to start my own business?

ANSWER:
Relax; you have plenty of time, and also lots of company. In fact, the SBA and AARP recently partnered up to put an emphasis on educating seniors about this exact matter. There are loads of opportunities.

Let's talk about this.

First off, unless you want to ride off into the sunset right now (and most of us don't), there are lots of reasons to start a business later in life. Check this: Ray Kroc started McDonald's at age 52. Harland Sanders franchised KFC when he was 64. Steve Jobs brought his greatest innovations to Apple in his late 40s. So it's not just the 20-somethings like Mark Zuckerberg who innovate and start businesses. OK, let's all say it together: "50 is the new 30."

According to a recent news release, the SBA and AARP are launching their strategic alliance to provide counseling and training to entrepreneurs over the age of 50 who want to start or grow a small business. The SBA offers online training courses and a nationwide network of SCORE business mentors and counselors. The two organizations expect to train 100,000 "encore entrepreneurs" — men and women over 50 who are starting or running small businesses.

SBA has set up a dedicated web page for Americans over 50. It features an excellent self-assessment tool to help potential small business owners understand their readiness for starting a business. There is also information to help with business planning, shaping a winning business idea, counseling, financial services, and finding local resources.

We need to be frank about the issue of elder employability. It is difficult in the current economy for an older candidate to find traditional employment. There's a general impression, often wrong, that older workers are too set in their ways, are probably overqualified, may resent reporting to someone younger, and have low-level tech skills. This is unfair and unspoken, but common.

Most of the public discussion recently has centered on things like how to prepare an attention-getting resume, tips for using employment websites, and job-hunting suggestions like networking. But after months or even years of trying, many seniors are deciding to look into starting their own businesses.

Here are five points of advice for starting a new business as a senior:

Do your homework. Don't just assume that a hobby or another interest of yours will be the basis for a successful business. You'll need to do research on the market for your products and services. In particular, who are your target customers or clients? What are their needs? How will you reach them? What is your competition?

Have a realistic timeline. Planning a business involves lots of goal setting and forecasting. Planning out a 15- or 20-year timeline when you're 30 is fine but for someone 50 or 60 or older, it's unrealistic. The lure of that special vacation or spending time with the grandkids may be strong.

Be realistic about your physical stamina and abilities. Some businesses, such as construction and landscaping, are inherently very demanding physically. As time goes on, this reality may require you to add staff who can step in to do the heavy lifting in your place.

Consider buying a franchise. In general, franchises have a couple of strong points that attract older folks:

- They are typically profitable much sooner than an independent business might be.

- They generally involve lots of standardization and simplification —
  of products, procedures, and marketing materials — and a strong
  brand awareness.

Be sure to read the franchise disclosure document carefully and talk to
current franchisees. Check out *unhappyfranchisee.com*.

Get good financial advice. A common and serious mistake is to plow all
of one's savings, retirement funds, 401(k) accounts, and then any other
assets into the business. While this is not advisable, you will of course have
some initial investment to put up, and it's likely you'll have to "feed" the
business for its initial months. Be sure you start with a written business
plan and fact-based financial projections. Also, it's best to have a stop-loss
strategy. This is where you define a future point at which, if necessary, you
will shut the business down rather than incur more losses.

"Silver startups" and "olderpreneurs" are getting some press. To explore
further, look into *sba.gov*, *score.org*, and *aarp.org/work/small business*.

STAGE TWO:
STARTUP

Here's where you pull the trigger. Focus on building your branding and customer base. Introduce your goods and services with appropriate promotion. Things you do right at this stage will have major impacts downstream.

Introductory Thoughts

- Research the market for your products and services. Pay special attention to your direct and indirect competition. Who are your customers and how will you reach them?

- Be aware of the basics of accounting and your financial progress as you launch. It's all about cash flow.

- If you need to hire employees, be very careful. This is a big step and needs great care.

- Revisit your business plan frequently.

- Expect to spend a great deal of your time on the business.

11 WHAT IS MY INTELLECTUAL PROPERTY, AND HOW DO I PROTECT IT?

> **QUESTION:**
> *A business advisor told me that I have intellectual property that is worthy of protection. What does this mean, and what should I do about it?*
>
> **ANSWER:**
> *Those familiar little symbols and abbreviations — TM, SM, Pat. Pend., and © — carry a lot of legal weight when it comes to safeguarding a company's proprietary names, designs, products, and services. Virtually every large firm has its intellectual property (IP) protected from misuse. As an entrepreneur, you should make sure your small business's valuable IP is protected as well.*
>
> *Let's talk about this.*

A **trademark** (TM) is not the same as a patent or copyright, though the differences are subtle. According to the U.S. Patent and Trademark Office (USPTO), a trademark is a word, name, symbol, or device used in business to indicate a source of the goods (i.e., your business). It also distinguishes your goods from those sold by any other business. Some common examples of trademarks are Ford, Velcro, and Frisbee.

A **service mark** (SM) is like a trademark, except that it identifies and distinguishes the source of a service rather than that of a product. Examples: Roto-Rooter, AT&T, and even the MGM lion's roar.

A **patent** for an invention grants a specific legal property right to the inventor — "the right to exclude others from making, using, offering for sale or selling" the same invention. That's typically a utility patent, which we see all around us. Be aware that there is a less stringent level of patent, called a design patent, that covers the appearance of an item as opposed to its internal construction or function. Your business may well have items with patentable designs.

But a word of caution is in order here. Though a patent is fine, it is not a guarantee that no one will try to breach it — with a legitimate claim to a similar invention or not. For some ugly stories on this, Google "patent troll" and see what you think.

A **copyright** (©) is a protection for authors of original works including literary, dramatic, musical, artistic, and other intellectual works, both published and unpublished.

The internet has transformed the process of applying for a trademark into something accessible to anyone willing to spend some time to understand the intricacies. But while you require no special legal knowledge to apply, the field is filled with potential pitfalls and wrong turns that could sabotage your trademark filing. For example, the application requires that you identify goods or services under specific categories. But misunderstanding these categories and filing too broadly or too narrowly can cause problems later on or even ruin your trademark. A qualified trademark attorney can help you avoid such problems.

Another interesting fact about secure IP is that the protection can be lost through generification. This occurs when a trademarked word becomes so commonly used that it becomes synonymous with the name of the product or service. Examples of some onetime trademarks that have been lost in the U.S., in some cases by big companies: aspirin (Bayer), dry ice, escalator (Otis Elevator), flip phone (Motorola), laundromat (Westinghouse), and linoleum. Some trademarks that have endured include Band-Aid; Formica, Jacuzzi, Kleenex, Play-Doh, and Q-tips. Their owners have held firm by stipulating, for example, "Kleenex brand facial tissue" in all their marketing.

A **trade secret** is another way to protect IP. Just as it sounds, the formula for the "special sauce" or whatever, is kept secret and known to few. Examples include: the formula for Coca-Cola (a secret since 1886. The formula is in a bank vault in Atlanta.); KFC's Original Recipe "11 herbs and spices"; the formula of WD-40; and the recipe for Hostess Twinkies. Unlike a patent or trademark, a trade secret doesn't expire unless it is discovered and made public.

The USPTO's website (*uspto.gov*) provides a wealth of information and resources about protecting your small business's IP. You'll find basic information about trademarks, patents, and copyrights, links to easy-to-follow guides, and search engines for researching existing trademarks and patents.

As a final thought, you may someday want to sell your business. It will be worth substantially more if a prospective buyer sees an array of valuable and protected IP.

12 I NEED HELP WITH MY DECISION-MAKING SKILLS

QUESTION:

In my small business, I'm OK with the technical aspects and pretty good with selling, but I'm not a trained manager. My decision-making skills are a bit weak and I tend to shoot from the hip. Are there some fundamental skills I could learn?

ANSWER:

Yes, there are, and you'll be happy to find out that the basics are pretty easy to add to your toolkit.

Let's talk about this.

For starters, take a look at exactly what types of decisions you need to make. Are they just routine day-to-day stuff, or are they huge, make-or-break types of issues? Let's define three different categories of decisions. The first group includes all the normal, everyday, ho-hum business issues and matters. You probably do this many times a day. For example, maybe it's time to replace a $100 printer, meet with a new sales rep, or upgrade your website. Depending on the size of your business, these may be decisions you can make and then delegate the implementation to others.

At the other extreme is a category of very complex decisions. Here is where the stakes are high. In some cases, you may even be "betting the company." Examples: moving your business to a new location, taking in a new business partner, or making a major change in a core product or service. For these biggies, there are numerous technical and quantitative ways to gather and analyze data and crunch the numbers.

For now, we'll focus on decisions in the middle group. These are the medium-importance decisions that have some long-term impact but don't risk breaking the bank. Examples: setting the marketing budget for next year, evaluating whether you need a new delivery van, or choosing how best to roll out a new product or service.

In making these decisions, it's best if you have an advisory board. This is much less formal than a board of directors. Typically, your advisors might be a group of four or five people with relevant business experience. They bring an outside perspective and a bit of "been there, done that" confidence. Good choices for your board might include a trusted mentor, a SCORE counselor, a retired banker or financial manager, or college faculty. Look for people who have technical or administrative knowledge in areas where you are weakest. Your commercial loan officer may not be willing to serve on your advisory board due to concern about lender liability exposure, but he or she could recommend a colleague or other businessperson as an advisor.

Management decision-making, like many other complex processes, is best mastered by breaking it down into smaller parts. There are numerous ways to do this. If you Google "business decision model," you'll find everything from the very simple (basically a coin flip) to the extremely complex (12-step methods with lots of technical and statistical involvement).

Here's a general method, using six steps to make effective decisions:

Define the objective. This should be in writing, and specific as to what the measurable outcome will be. Gather the board and get everyone in agreement on the goal. What would success look like? When will we see it? How will we measure it?

Research the facts. If you're evaluating an opportunity, what are the likely costs and benefits? If you're solving a problem, when did it start and what are some possible causes?

Generate some possible options and solutions. Here's where techniques like brainstorming and "what if-ing" are useful. Also realize that some of your decisions will have legal and accounting implications. If you aren't sure where you stand, ask with your lawyer or accountant for guidance before you go further.

Narrow down to a few good alternatives. Explore these and choose the best one. For many managers, the toughest step is closing off information gathering and moving toward an actionable plan. This hesitation can lead to "analysis paralysis". For most businesses, a decision made promptly on good information is better than one made too late or not at all. As Voltaire said, "Don't let the perfect be the enemy of the good."

Communicate your decision, and take action. Make sure that everyone involved sees what's coming, and then implement the decision.

Evaluate the results, and modify your decision if needed. Be sure to include this important feedback step in your planning. In a very innovative business, you might hear the phrase "ready, fire, aim." This allows for the fact that your first shot might miss the mark.

This six-step method is easy to learn and is flexible. Try it and see if it helps you out.

13 ACCOUNTING BASICS

QUESTION:

I took an accounting class some years back but I think I need a tune-up on bookkeeping and accounting for my new business. Also, what outside professional services are available and how will I know when I need them?

ANSWER:

Well, those are good questions for any young business to know about.

Let's talk about this.

We'll look at a grab bag of things to know about small business bookkeeping and accounting. Also, we'll examine the increasing role accounting plays in your business as you grow. But relax — no stuffy terms like amortization or retained earnings today.

You know, of course, that your business has to keep records of your financial activity. For starters, these must be sufficient to provide a basis for accurate reporting on your income tax return. But correct and reliable information about how your business is doing is even more valuable to you. This allows you to compare your actual performance to your business plan and to make decisions about how to run your business. If you don't have a written business plan, contact SCORE for a free and confidential appointment and get help with this important matter.

If you're new to business, go to the IRS website (*irs.gov*), click on the "Forms & Instructions" tab, and search for and download a Schedule C. This is the form you will need to fill out and include with your next personal income tax return. It shows you the different categories of expenses you will need to use.

While you're there, the IRS has a very well written pamphlet on this exact topic. Its Publication 583, *Starting a Business and Keeping Records.* At the IRS website, enter "583" in the search box, and scroll down a bit to download the PDF. You can also get a printed copy at your local IRS office.

A very small business can get away with checkbook accounting. This is where all revenues are deposited into the business account and all expenses are paid out of that same account. Don't be stingy with space in the check register — be sure that you enter ample information for each check entry about the payee and the purpose of the expense. At year-end, you may not remember why you wrote that check to the Fred Carlson Company unless you noted that it was for office supplies.

More established businesses may benefit from using accounting software to keep things organized. Accounting packages are helpful and user-friendly (forget the old stuff about debits and credits). There are some free programs that are pretty good that you can find on the internet. The step above free programs would, of course, be QuickBooks, the de facto standard for small business accounting. It's available in several versions, and there are excellent training videos on YouTube.

As most companies grow, they need some help with the books — perhaps a simple monthly summary of sales and expenses. As soon as you hire employees, the game changes. Unless you have idle time and the inclination, you're better off using an outside service to process the payroll and prepare all the required quarterly reports than trying to handle it yourself.

Some businesses grow enough to need in-house bookkeeping staff. This might mean a part- or full-time bookkeeper to post transactions, write checks, and handle other functions. A full-charge bookkeeper has additional duties, perhaps preparing monthly or quarterly financial statements. A business at this stage will typically use an outside accountant to do the year-end books. If your business is a corporation, there will also be a separate income tax return to prepare.

Next up the scale is to bring the accounting function fully in-house. This allows a business to prepare budgets, do financial analyses, and make decisions about things like pricing and cash flow planning.

Let's do a quick review of some common accounting credentials:

- A registered tax return preparer (RTRP), a recent designation, is one who is IRS-qualified to prepare tax returns for compensation.

- A certified public accountant (CPA) is licensed by the state to perform accounting work, including audits. This is a high-level credential.

- A certified managerial accountant (CMA) focuses on the internal operations of the business and how they can be improved.

- Other, less common credentials include enrolled agent (EA), certified fraud examiner (CFE), and certified internal auditor (CIA).

Last thought: it's best to work with a professional who is familiar with your type of business. Ask other businesspeople to recommend an accountant they use.

14 BUSINESS CARD BASICS

QUESTION:

I'm concerned that our business cards look outdated and unprofessional. So I'm wondering: With all the current emphasis on internet marketing and social media, do we even need cards anymore?

ANSWER:

Yes, you sure do. A professional business card is an important part of your company's overall image. They're inexpensive and you can print them in small quantities. Cards can even be tailored to your different customer types.

Let's talk about this.

Before we look at the role of business cards in modern life, we'll first look at how it came to be that we even have business cards.

In France in the 1700s, people of class sent a "visiting card" ahead to notify someone that they would be visiting. Of course communication at that time was very basic, largely by delivered on horseback. The typical card was about the size of a playing card, bearing just the person's name, and the nicer ones were engraved. This practice spread to England in the 1800s. There was a great deal of formality about how the calling card was presented. This included very specific social rules about which corner of the card, if any, was folded forward. Each of the corner folds signified a different purpose for the visit. For example, folding down the upper-left corner signified that you, the visitor, wanted to convey congratulations. Folding the lower-left corner signaled that you wanted to bring condolences. If the recipient returned the card to the sender, it meant "No, thank you."

As time went on, immigrants brought the card presentation idea to America, and we adopted it. Cards here were smaller and more likely to bear a business reference of some kind.

Clearly, the role of business cards has evolved. Now, much more business interaction is conducted face-to-face. Your website is your extended card. In fact, it's pretty common now to have an initial, and then even an ongoing, business relationship with someone you've never actually met. So it may be time to take a look, not just at your cards, but at the whole image your business presents to the world.

The first thing to do is to unify the design of all your graphics. This is an important part of what's called your "branding." The branding notion is fairly recent. It's a marketing concept that suggests you should unify and standardize the appearance of your logo, signage, web presence, and everything that visually brings your business to mind.

In designing your cards, it's probably best to stick with a few basics:

- U.S. cards are typically 3.5 x 2.0 inches.
- The font should be clear and ample in size.
- Color printing costs a bit more but is very effective.
- Consider a folding card if you can really use more room.
- Fun, creative cards are much more memorable than ho-hum cards.

Here are some ideas to get you going.

Full-service local print shops. Ask around. Most every city has several good full-service printers. These have on-staff design professionals who will work with you to coordinate all of your graphics and visuals. They can also suggest ideas that are specific to your business — for example, printing your mission statement, a map to your store, or a space for a client's next appointment on the back of the card.

Online printing sources. *Vistaprint.com* offers 100 high-quality cards at a modest cost with free shipping. *Moo.com* and *businesscards24.com* and others have similar offers. Basic design templates are available for you to fill in as you wish.

Print your own. You can also print your own business cards, as few as ten at a time. You can do the layout work in templates available in Microsoft Word. Also, Avery now makes cardstock for printing good quality cards. Most of the older cardstock looked cheap but the newer products are thicker and snap apart, leaving clean edges. Free software is available at their website, *avery.com.*

Also, it's fine to carry more than one type of card. For example, you might attend a social event where your business contact information (office phone and email, etc.) is not appropriate. A social-business card is the trick in this situation. Suggestion: use a different design or paper color to keep track of which is which.

And here's the latest news: several free smartphone apps are available that allow you to scan a received card and pull its information directly into your contacts database.

My wild prediction? In five years, your business card may be a QR code on your thumbnail.

15 WHEN SHOULD I HIRE MY FIRST EMPLOYEE?

QUESTION:
My business is growing and I'm considering hiring my first employee. What do I need to know?

ANSWER:
Bringing on your first employee marks a major and fundamental change in your business. All sorts of new challenges come along with being a new employer.

Let's talk about this.

First, why do you think you need an employee? Be specific and realistic. Are sales up? Are you turning orders away, and not just seasonally? Will this growth continue? Are there new areas of sales opportunities that you can't address by yourself?

If so, fine. What you need is someone with complementary skill sets. Some examples of this are technical skills if you're tech-shy, sales ability if you're not a good salesperson, and creativity if you're not so inclined. But if you just need someone to occasionally bounce ideas off, then join a local business group like your chamber of commerce or a more specialized group close to your field of business — for example, a technology-related group. Also, remember that you can contact SCORE or your local Small Business Development Center.

Second, note that there are several alternatives to full-on hiring. Some smaller tasks are appropriate for interns. Local temporary employment firms will "rent" you employees, as needed. Depending on your business, you might be able to use independent contractors (ICs), who are not employees.

But caution with ICs! Be sure to check with your state's department of labor and the IRS (*irs.gov*) on their requirements for having a genuine IC relationship that will pass scrutiny. Briefly, it's important that ICs have their own business. This means, for example, that they have a business license, keep their own books, use their own tools, perform similar work for others, and generally control their own work. On the other hand, if you have substantial control over what, when, how, and where the people work, they are employees, regardless of what you say.

If you are considering a part-timer, remember to look into job share programs. Google "job sharing for employers" and see what applies to your situation.

To prepare for hiring, consider the following:

- Can you afford the employee's wages, benefits, and payroll taxes?
- Did your business plan foresee adding an employee at this stage? If not, then exactly what changed?
- Do you have a clear interviewing and selection process ready to use? Are you ready to be an effective supervisor?
- Do you know at least the basics of labor law?
- Do you have a suitable employee policy manual, or can you find one online?
- Are you familiar with payroll preparation, and do you have a system or the software to handle it? If not, you will definitely need outside help.
- What workspace, equipment, and other items will the employee need?
- Do you have the necessary accounts set up with the federal government and the various state agencies?
- Can you commit to ongoing training and incentives for your employee?

This is a very good time to have a brief chat with each of your advisory board members — your accountant, legal advisor, banker, insurance professional, and others whom you trust.

It is also a time for a bit of introspection. Are you ready to give up some of your authority? That's what delegation requires. Many entrepreneurs have trouble with this.

Last thought: if your need to hire is because you're upsizing from a home business to an outside place of business, be extremely careful. These are two of the most challenging small business changes and are loaded with pitfalls when attempted together.

16 WHAT IS A SWOT ANALYSIS?

QUESTION:
Someone told me that I should look into doing a "SWOT analysis" of my business. What does that mean, and is this some goofy fringe idea or a real thing?

ANSWER:
A SWOT analysis is a common and valid analytical tool for business planning and decision-making. It's straightforward, very helpful, and something you should be aware of.

Let's talk about this.

To start off, SWOT is an acronym for **S**trengths, **W**eaknesses, **O**pportunities, and **T**hreats. We'll discuss each of these shortly. First, you need to have a sense of where a SWOT analysis fits and how you might use it.

A SWOT analysis is a tool for evaluating a business idea, plan, or opportunity. It can also help you get your arms around a major business decision. And even better, there are excellent free templates complete with suggestions and instructions available on the internet (*businessballs.com* and *mindtools.com/rs/swot*) that will have you up and running in just a few minutes.

This isn't some recent fad. The SWOT concept originated from research conducted at Stanford Research Institute (now SRI International) in the 1960s. Large firms, including many Fortune 500 companies, funded the research. This study sprang from their need to find out why their corporate strategic planning efforts had mostly failed. The surprising result was that the SWOT analysis arose as a simpler, better, and more effective way to make strategic business decisions.

A SWOT analysis always starts with a clearly defined objective, a desired end state, or a defined condition. Some situations for using it might be starting a new business, taking on a new product line, marketing to a different target group, or evaluating the state of your service delivery.

Two of the four elements of SWOT are for internal factors (your business's strengths and weaknesses), and two evaluate external factors (opportunities and threats.) We'll look at the elements briefly and then go through an example SWOT analysis.

Strengths. You list your strengths relative to the competition. These could include a better location, staff, product mix, reputation, or whatever makes up your business advantage.

Weaknesses. This is a time to be realistic and honest. The analysis of weaknesses in your organization looks at situations where your business does not measure up. This suggests that competitors have an advantage over you. But do realize that a known problem is better than an unknown one.

Opportunities. This refers to external factors, like a growing market segment or a joint venture, that could provide additional future growth or other benefits.

Threats. These are outside factors, like new competitors or impending negative legislation, that could hinder you in achieving your business objectives and goals.

OK, let's have some fun with an example of a simple SWOT analysis. Let's say Nicole wants to buy an existing retail floral shop. As part of her business plan to apply for bank financing, she has done a SWOT analysis.

Strengths:

- It's an existing and successful location.
- Nicole has a degree in horticulture.

- Two experienced employees are staying on.
- Nicole's mother is a wedding planner and a likely source of new business.
- The business has an exclusive supply contract with a major vendor.

Weaknesses:

- Nicole has no direct management experience.
- The refrigeration equipment is old and energy-inefficient.
- The website is not backed by a social media presence.
- The floral delivery division needs a new van and image.
- The inventory control systems are outmoded.

Opportunities:

- Nearby businesses are thriving and willing to do co-promotions.
- New packaging products enable shipping fresh flowers widely.
- One competitor is shutting down for personal reasons and will give Nicole his customer list.
- A proposed downtown business improvement zone bodes well.

Threats:

- Many local grocers are expanding their floral departments.
- Internet floral purchases are growing.
- Some exotic flower species are not available to Nicole's shop.
- Several competitors run aggressive loss leaders.
- A stagnant economy could depress discretionary purchases.

As you can see, a SWOT analysis isn't something that you knock out in one 30-minute session, especially if the issues are complex.

Hopefully this adds another tool to your business management toolkit.

17 JOB INTERVIEWING NO-NOS

QUESTION:
I'll need to add some employees soon. I hear that there are some topics and questions to avoid in conducting job interviews. Is this something I should be aware of?

ANSWER:
Absolutely. Certain topics are completely off-limits, and it may surprise you how mild some of these are.

Let's talk about this.

Hiring decisions are critical to your business success. There are two types of hiring errors: hiring someone you shouldn't have and not hiring a candidate you should have. You may find it difficult to make good hiring decisions when there are so many topics you can't legally discuss.

Typically, a job seeker will fill out some type of an application, probably offer a resume and a cover letter, and then, upon your invitation, appear for an in-person interview. The off-limits rules apply to the entire process. In short, the best way to avoid trouble is to ask questions about the applicant's skills and ability to do the job rather than questions about the applicant.

Let's review some categories, with examples of illegal and legal questions:

- **National origin**

   Illegal: Where were you born? Are you a U.S. citizen? Is English your native language?

   OK: Do you speak Spanish fluently? (But only if that is actually a part of the job.) Also OK: Are you authorized to work in the U.S.?

- **Marital status and family issues**

  Illegal: Are you married? Do you have children? Are you considering having children?

  OK: Questions about the candidate's ability to meet work schedules such as evenings, on-call duty, or out-of-town travel.

- **Age**

  Illegal: How old are you? When were you born? What year did you graduate from high school? Were you in college during the 1990s?

  OK: Are you over 18?

- **Personal statistics**

  Illegal: How tall are you? How much do you weigh? Are you in good health?

  OK: Specific questions about a job duty (e.g., Can you lift a 40-pound carton and carry it 100 feet?).

- **Credit history**

  Illegal: How is your credit score? Have you ever filed bankruptcy or been foreclosed upon?

  OK: Are you bondable? (But only if the job has cash-handling duties or other financial responsibility.)

- **Religion**

  Illegal: What religious holidays do you observe?

  OK: Specific questions about work availability (e.g., Friday nights or weekends).

- **Disability**

  Illegal: Do you have any disabilities or chronic illnesses?

  OK: Are you able to perform the duties of this job?

- **Criminal background**

  Illegal: Have you ever been arrested?

  OK: Have you ever been convicted of a crime related to this line of business.

- **Military service**

  Illegal: Were you honorably discharged?

  OK: What relevant training and skills did you acquire in the military?

It is nearly always **illegal** to ask a question about race, gender, national origin, appearance, age, sexual orientation, health, or disability. There are exceptions but the burden is on you to show why the question is valid and job-related. The term for this is a bona-fide occupational qualification, often referred to as a BFOQ. Much of this law dates back to Title VII of the Civil Rights Act of 1964.

Examples of BFOQ situations: an airline can enforce a mandatory retirement age for pilots. A Catholic school can lawfully require that an applicant for principal be Catholic. A warehouse business could require an applicant to be able to place a 30-pound item on a six-foot-high shelf and retrieve it. According to the Civil Rights Act of 1964, a BFOQ must be "reasonably necessary to the normal operation of a particular business." Don't expect the BFOQ exception to cover many circumstances.

The Americans with Disabilities Act requires that you make "reasonable accommodations" for an applicant or employee with a disability. Examples would be removing barriers or raising the height of a desk so a person using a wheelchair could navigate. Someone with a visual impairment might request stronger workspace lighting. Your business must meet these reasonable accommodations unless "to do so would cause undue hardship." Bear in mind that accommodating those with disabilities opens up a huge new pool of labor.

A good practice is to follow a written checklist for your interviews. This will help you stick to the legal topics. It is also helpful in making sure, and demonstrating, if need be, that you ask similar questions of all candidates.

Labor law is very complex. It changes over time, through both legislation and court interpretation. Some laws apply to certain businesses but not to others. Penalties for discrimination are harsh. Watch for the tripwires, and get knowledgeable legal help if you need it.

18 DO I NEED AN EMPLOYEE HANDBOOK?

QUESTION:

I'm starting to interview and hire new employees. Several of them have asked to see our employee handbook and I don't have one. What do I need to know about this? Is it a phony feel-good thing or something I actually need to have?

ANSWER:

Sooner or later, you will need to have one. An employee handbook (by other names, it may be a policies and procedures manual, staff guidebook, or employee manual) is becoming a necessity, though maybe for the wrong reasons.

Let's talk about this.

First, we'll discuss a recommended tone to take in your employee handbook, Then we'll outline what topics to include, some precautions, a few examples of difficult situations with employees, and some sources of information you can access to create your employee handbook without stepping into legal trouble.

To the extent possible, your handbook should be worded in the positive. No employee, whether new to the company or not, will be excited and motivated by a whole bunch of restrictions and heavy-handed "don'ts." Clearly, there will be sections that have to be worded in the negative — for example, prohibiting illegal drugs in the workplace. However, try to keep the tone upbeat and empowering.

Here is a model for a typical small business employee handbook with four sample topics for each section.

Introduction. This section should welcome the employee and give some context and background for their information. Possible topics:

- Your mission statement
- What your business stands for
- A brief history of the business
- A few key products or services

Employment policies. This begins the "nuts and bolts" of the document. Typical issues:

- The hiring process
- Nondiscrimination policy
- Probation or orientation period
- Employee evaluations

Standards of conduct. Here, you'll mention things like these:

- Dress codes
- Absence and lateness
- Customer/client relations
- Discharge

Computer and technology issues. No surprise: this area is evolving quickly.

- Use of company technology
- Use of personal devices at work
- Protection of company information
- Internet and social media guidelines

Safety, security, and training. Example topics:

- Safety of employees, guests, and others (top concern)
- Use of the company suggestion box

- OSHA and state occupational safety and health laws
- In-house training opportunities; tuition reimbursement program

Drug and alcohol policies. Example topics:

- Prohibition of possession or use of illegal drugs
- Prohibition of alcohol consumption before or at work
- Requirement to report suspected violations to management
- Zero-tolerance and immediate discharge policies

Legal requirements. Example topics:

- Family Medical Leave Act
- Equal employment and nondiscrimination policies
- Notice that this document is not a contract
- At-will status reminder

Unfortunately, many workplace rules are driven by defensive legal issues — fear of lawsuits and claims of things like employment discrimination, sexual harassment, unlawful discharge, or retaliation. Most large businesses, and nearly all governmental agencies and departments, require each employee to sign a statement that they have read and understand the contents of the employee handbook and agree to abide by it.

Employment law is changing very quickly and there are lots of traps for the uninformed. Imagine yourself in these four situations (all of which actually happened):

- You discover that an employee has been sending sexually offensive emails from a company computer. When disciplined, the employee claims an expectation of privacy since it was his personal email account.
- An employee is acting very strangely at the job. There is clear suspicion of drug use but she refuses a test. You discharge her. She sues.
- An employee posts, from home, some very derogatory comments about your company on his Facebook page. When disciplined, he claims free-speech rights.

- An at-will employee (this means either you or the employee can terminate the relationship at any time) claims that your employee handbook made some enforceable job promises. The Washington Supreme Court ruled in 1984 that under certain conditions, the employer's at-will rights may be modified by promises in an employee manual (Thompson v. St. Regis Paper Co.).

If you operate a fairly small business and feel comfortable drawing up your own employee handbook, give it a go. You can get some help online:

- Google "free employee handbook template."
- The SBA has a great list of what to consider and include in your handbook here: *sba.gov/content/employee-handbooks*
- Try *rocketlawyer.com* for another customizable template.

Strongly consider running your draft by an employment law attorney. It's worth the couple hundred bucks to make sure you're on the right track.

19 MARKET RESEARCH BASICS

> **QUESTION:**
> *I've been told that I need to do some market research. My business is young and small and I really don't know much about this. Can you give me some basics?*
>
> **ANSWER:**
> *Yes; unless you have tons of money and can afford to market blindly, your best bet is to do some research and find out about your market base.*
>
> *Let's talk about this.*

We'll look into some central concepts of market research, some terms you should know a bit about, several examples of specific market research techniques, and some helpful information sources.

A main objective of market research is to define and identify your **target market:** who are your likely customers or clients? What specific groups of people might be interested in your goods and/or services? You will use this information to prepare a **marketing strategy**, which details how you will reach those customers and encourage them to buy.

The older market segmentation term "market demographic" has now become "market psychographic." This means that you're looking at defining your market into segments based on their different personality traits, values, attitudes, interests, and lifestyles. Here's the difference: let's say we have a 54 year-old male — that would be his demographic, period. But he could be a single guy, a husband and father of two, or a grandfather of four — all of whom have very different psychographics. Segmentation allows you to focus your marketing on the target markets you want to reach.

One extremely important function of market research is that it compels you to direct your attention to the wants and needs of your customers. You can't focus just on your products and services themselves.

Consider this: say you have a unique product but no sales yet. If you have a product fixation, you'll conclude that it's time to jump right into advertising and selling it. But hold on, you're looking through the wrong end of the telescope. If you have a market orientation, you will realize that your effort is better spent on finding out who has a "felt need" for your product or service.

Market research has multiple applications:

- For a new business, it's an essential component — and one of the most important — of your written business plan.

- An existing business, when considering adding a new product or service, needs to know how best to launch it successfully.

- An active, growing business should always be looking at new markets. This could be a different geographic market, like exporting on the internet, or a new psychographic market, like selling to early-career millennials.

- A mature business needs to adapt and refresh its offerings to change with the times.

Data is categorized by source as primary or secondary. **Primary data** is information you generate. Examples: a customer survey you conduct, a focus group you arrange, a comparative analysis of your competitors' websites. Three big advantages of primary data are that it is very current, it is more specific, and it can be tailored to your business's particular needs. The main disadvantage is that it costs more than using existing data.

Secondary data is information you get from existing outside sources. Examples: department of revenue sales figures, information from a trade organization about industry trends, business information from one of the public library's online databases. Two big advantages of secondary data are that it is readily available and usually free. The tradeoff is that it may be dated or too broad geographically to be relevant.

The two types of data are qualitative and quantitative. **Qualitative data** is easy to generate: just ask someone a question and note their answer. An example would be a retail store surveying customers about their satisfaction or product preferences. Or a service business might ask customers to comment on its pricing compared to the competition. It's more conversational than statistical.

Quantitative data is expressed in numbers. Research to generate quantitative data can be simple, like a phone survey of your local market. Example: "About how much would you be willing to pay for [describe your product]?" Or it can be very involved, like the rigorous research a retail chain conducts before choosing a new location.

A major asset for your market research is your local library system. Here's the scoop: look into the system's online databases, many of which are subscription-only and have private information not available on the internet or to the general public.

For more information, Google "small business market research tips." For a good overview of information sources, go to *score.org* and enter "market research" in the search box. Also check out *marketresearch.com* and *knowthis.com*.

20 INEXPENSIVE MARKETING TIPS

QUESTION:
My marketing budget is very limited. How can I get the biggest bang for the buck?

ANSWER:
There are some techniques you should know about. We're all buried in information overload so it takes some knowledge and creativity to get above the noise level.

Let's talk about this.

It's very good that you're working with a marketing budget. Many small businesses just muddle through the year without a plan and then later realize they overspent or didn't get the impact they wanted ... or even worse, both.

Here's an interesting backstory. Retailing pioneer John Wanamaker was way ahead of his time in Philadelphia in the 1870s. He originated the department store concept, introduced the notion of house brands, and came up with the idea of price tags. In 1874, he printed the first-ever, copyrighted store advertisement. Later, he opened the first in-store restaurant in 1876 and installed electric lights in 1878. He also coined the term and offered the first "white sale." But note this: he's actually most famous for his comment "Half the money I spend on advertising is wasted. The trouble is, I don't know which half."

When you set up your marketing budget for the year, you'll probably earmark a certain percentage of your projected sales. For example, an established retail store might expect to spend 5–8 percent of sales on marketing. A young service business may need to devote 15 or even 20 percent. These expenses should include all your advertising, promotion, website maintenance, local events, giveaways, marketing materials, and other costs. Before you set a number, think about three things:

- **Your stage in the market:** are you a startup, emerging, stable, or dominant?
- **Your direct and indirect competition:** are they aggressive or much larger than you?
- **Your profit margins:** what can you reasonably afford to spend?

Many businesses that buy and then resell goods from others have access to what's called "co-op advertising money." This is a reimbursement that a vendor offers to a reseller for running advertising that gives the vendor prominent mention. For example, an appliance store might run an ad for a major national brand item. The upside: you get to promote your business largely on the other guy's dime. The downside: there are some hoops to jump through.

To get you started, here are ten examples of low-cost marketing methods. See which might be adaptable for your business.

1. **Give a free talk or seminar.** Lots of local service groups are delighted to have a guest present a topic of interest to their members. Some examples: book clubs, neighborhood meetings, garden clubs, Rotary Clubs, church groups.

2. **Distribute attractive flyers.** Have some colorful half-page flyers printed, and hire someone to hand them out where people congregate. Do not put them on windshields; in many cities, that's considered littering. Provide a limited-time coupon, special offer, or other reason for customers to visit you soon.

3. **Generate some testimonials.** Offer your goods or services to selected people at a reduced price in return for favorable statements about their satisfaction. These are especially effective in a short video on your website or YouTube.

4. **Cross-promote with other businesses.** Find other businesses that target and address your same market segments — but of course with different, complementary products and services.

5. **Attend social networking events.** Many chambers of commerce offer these and are very active in this regard. Go to your chamber's website and click on the "Events" tab. Take a big stack of business cards and any other promotional literature you have.

6. **Issue a media release.** When your business has a newsworthy event like an anniversary or a significant new product or service, put the word out. Get some help on this so you come off professionally and, as a business, be who your target market segment would want to seek out.

7. **Build an email newsletter following.** For starters, look into *constantcontact.com* and similar services that allow you to greatly leverage your marketing effort. But beware; you'll have to deliver frequent original, high-quality content, not just fluff.

8. **Cosponsor a local sports team.** This is an inexpensive and effective way to build a local presence.

9. **Set up Google Alerts.** These alert you to internet searches for particular terms that you've preregistered.

10. **Reward your existing customers and clients for referrals.** There's no easier way to get new customers than from your existing clientele.

A fun bit of history: the concept of guerrilla marketing — getting big results on a small budget — was coined by Jay Conrad Levinson in his book *Guerrilla Marketing*, first published in 1983. It was an instant hit. An excellent fourth edition came out in 2007, too early to have full inclusion of the internet. For the latest, Google "Guerrilla marketing" for hundreds of inexpensive marketing ideas.

STAGE THREE:
GROWTH

WOW! You're up and running! This stage — especially if it's rapid growth — requires a great deal of your attention and focus, and a full-time commitment. Keep very aware of your competition, both brick and mortar and online. It's also a good time to check in with your advisory board and give a progress report.

Introductory Thoughts

- You should become profitable (exceed breakeven in sales). If you are not profitable, reexamine your business plan to see if you're off track or need to change some of your assumptions or projections.

- Closely monitor your financial results, at least monthly. Things change quickly.

- This is a good time to look ahead, specifically to how you will transition to maturity. What has worked? What didn't?

- Keep in mind your work-life balance. Set aside some time for family and friends.

- Expect to spend a great deal of your time on the business.

21 MARKETING NO-NOS

QUESTION:

I feel like my business is wobbling along in a marketing fog. I've tried quite a few different forms of advertising and promotion. Some seem to work while others don't. What's the deal?

ANSWER:

It's very common for a small business to struggle with creative ways to attract new customers and clients. There are lots of traps along the way.

Let's talk about this.

First off, realize that marketing is as much art as it is science. This has been true for a long time. Consider this: a pioneer in retailing, John Wanamaker, opened one of the nation's first department stores in Philadelphia in the 1860s. He said, "Half the money I spend on advertising is wasted. The trouble is, I don't know which half."

Let's take a look at ten common and costly **marketing mistakes** that small business owners make.

1. **Not having a solid marketing plan.** This is the single biggest reason why businesses, like yours, wobble along. Remember the old saying from Alice in Wonderland: If you don't know where you're going, any road will take you there.

   If you have a written business plan, you probably included a discussion of your marketing plan and methods in it. The marketing plan lays out your roadmap, typically for a year. But even more than that, for most businesses it's the single most important section of your business plan. Just ask any commercial loan officer who's considering making a business loan, especially to a startup business.

There's a new way to customize your business's marketing plan, easily and for free. We'll talk about this more in a moment, but for now, let's move on.

2. **Overlooking your existing customers and clients.** Studies show that it costs ten or more times as much to attract a new customer as it does to reach out to an existing one.

3. **Having a confused pricing model.** You, as a new or small business, are NOT going to be the low-price leader, period. Especially in retail, the buyers for the big chains buy in mega-quantities. If you mention your pricing policies at all, be very careful what you are suggesting. Price matching with large competitors is a very bad idea.

4. **Spreading your advertising budget too thinly.** A common mistake is to allocate, say, 10 percent of your budget to each of ten different media. It's better to focus on three or four, and track the results.

5. **Failing to target your marketing to specific customer groups.** Especially for a startup, your marketing dollars are best spent by focusing on one or just a few subgroups. This might be a demographic niche or a group of prospects likely to want your products or services. For example, an upscale restaurant would get a higher return from advertising in a visitors' guide than in a college newspaper.

6. **Not having a killer website and a very strong social media presence.** This is so basic now that it goes without saying.

7. **Not testing the effectiveness of your marketing.** Look into a technique called "split run" or "A/B testing." It's simple and effective. You may have heard a TV or radio ad telling you something like "Go to *delta7.com*, that's delta and the number seven, to get this special price." The imaginary Delta Company has coded several websites to test which ads, or air times, produce the best results.

8. **Fearing repetition.** Marketing experts agree that customers respond after multiple advertising exposures.

9. **Arbitrary budgeting.** Most every type of business has at least one trade organization. These collect data from their members and can suggest what a typical marketing budget should be as a percentage of gross sales. For example, a retail business might devote 6 percent of sales to its marketing efforts, while a service business may devote 10 percent.

10. **Underusing public relations.** Volunteer to talk about your products or services on a radio show. Send out media releases when there's a noteworthy happening, like an upcoming event or new product unveiling.

If you need help with a marketing plan, the national SCORE organization has an excellent 64-page *Marketing Cookbook* for this exact purpose. You can print it out or browse the table of contents for what fits your needs. Google "SCORE Marketing Cookbook" to check this out.

22 BASICS OF SELLING

QUESTION:
My small business is doing OK but I think my weak selling skills are holding back growth. Are there some simple ways for me to improve my sales techniques?

ANSWER:
Sales and marketing skills are always valuable, whether you're promoting a product, a service, or an idea. There are loads of ways to improve your abilities.

Let's talk about this.

First, before you jump into a 10-week, $1,500 super-duper sales training course, make sure your product knowledge is up to speed. This means you must have a thorough understanding of your goods and services. Plus, you must also be confident about conveying this knowledge to others.

Second, do a little research into outside and local sources of help. A trade magazine relevant to your business may have helpful ideas on sales and marketing techniques. There are thousands of online sites and webinars. To start, Google "sales training" and see what might suit your needs. *Entrepreneur* magazine and its website (*entrepreneur.com*) are excellent. The SBA (*sba.gov*) and SCORE (*score.org*) websites have lots of material.

You might sit in on a few Toastmasters club meetings (most every city has several). Try to find a mentor or coach. Your local library has numerous books with selling and marketing information; look on the shelves around call number 658. And yes, there actually is a Boy Scout merit badge for Salesmanship.

Third, let's explore a selling technique that has been around for decades. It's having a resurgence and the likely reason is that we're all operating on information overload. It's simple (just four steps), and it's ethical and powerful. Its commonly known as the A-I-D-A method. These letters capture the stages a person goes through in making a buying decision: Attention, Interest, Desire, and Action. Here's how it works:

Attention. This is the critical first step. You must be visible. Until you have someone's attention, there is no point in going further. You have to get yourself, your ad, your jingle, or your message noticed. Effective attention-getting examples include the GEICO Gecko, flashing signage, and those bold tabloid headlines and magazine photos in the checkout line. There is so much competing junk and noise in our everyday lives that a presentation that doesn't grab attention in the first few seconds is lost.

Remember that most of our sensory input is visual and auditory. That's why the grade-school exercise is called "show and tell."

Interest. Once you have your prospect's attention, you need to deliver a message that will pique his or her interest. In marketing, this is called "baiting the hook," for obvious reasons. Basically, you mention or offer something that engages the person and generates interest. This is the time to mention the features and benefits of what you offer. Be specific.

Also, here's where the power words get big play. SALE! FREE! LIMITED TIME OFFER! BIG DISCOUNT! Or, more subtly, "15 minutes could save you 15 percent."

But wait, there's more. If you can offer an engaging visual of some kind, a testimonial, a sample, or some other attraction that appeals to your prospect or target market, then all the better.

Desire. OK, you have their attention and interest; now it's time to help them conclude that they want what you offer. A sense of urgency may be helpful. Remember that people always have choices, and so you must make dealing with you become the right choice. The best way to do this is to (1) remind them how you meet their needs or desires, and (2) get them to agree that you do.

At this step, it's essential that you read the prospect carefully. Try to get some feedback on the person's state of mind about the purchase. You can do this by signaling that you are done presenting and asking a question. This moves you into step four.

Action. If you think your prospect is ready for closing, you could simply ask a trial closing question like "What do you think? Is this what you're looking for?" Here's where your role is to listen. Your prospect will tell you where he or she is.

Always have a few fallback positions ready. For example, if the prospect says, "No, I'm not ready to buy," then an appropriate response might be "Could I send you some additional literature on the product?" Or, "May I call you next week to discuss our services further?"

And last, realize that most of what we've discussed about in-person selling applies to your work with advertising media too. The A-I-D-A method has broad application to nearly any type of persuasion. It's effective for phone sales, it can help you create your print materials, your on-air (broadcast) presence, and your online identity. And it's basic and easy to remember.

Sell on!

23 I'M IN RETAIL. HELP!

QUESTION:
My local retail business is facing some challenges. I want it — and me — to succeed, but I'm pretty naive about this. Can you give me some insight to help me understand retailing?

ANSWER:
To say that you're "facing some challenges" is a nice way to put it. Retailing at every scale and level has never been more challenging. Retail bankruptcies are in the news all the time. The key word is "adapt."

Let's talk about this.

Things are changing rapidly. Pretty much everybody in retail business needs to be at their top of their game. Let's start with the obvious threat: online competition, which has a fraction of the overhead of your physical brick and mortar store. To make matters more difficult, your relatively small store competes with many internet sellers with high sales volumes. They probably buy in quantities you can't get near, and thus they get big-lot pricing you can't even dream about.

And ... it gets worse. Some consumers go to their local retail stores to look at products in the flesh but then actually buy the goods online. Retailers call this "being a showroom for Amazon," and they hate it. Not only does it tie up unproductive inventory dollars, it uses your displays and sales staff time with no return. For retail stores offering small, easy-to-ship, high-value items like personal electronics, this is a big problem and a clear game changer.

Also, it's becoming common to see a shopper in a store using a mobile device to read an item's bar code. The app gives the user instant access to info on the best pricing near you, using the phone's GPS.

Here's some background. For most of the 1900s, we Americans patronized our local retail stores, which were mostly all in our downtowns at this time. This included not just routine shopping for groceries and the bulk of our daily needs, but even the purchase of a car, furniture, and other major items. In smaller towns, this continued into the 1970s or 1980s. But by then, most cities had attracted developers who built shopping malls. These drew the major anchor retailers, and then many others, away from the downtowns and into their shiny new spaces. The predictable "retail flight" left many downtowns with numerous storefronts that were vacant for years.

But now a new phase has begun. All across the nation, shopping malls are adapting away from retail spaces. As stores close, many of the spaces are refilling with non-retail uses like service businesses.

Many experts think retailing needs to discard an anachronism that has run its course. This is the $X.99 pricing tradition. Is $19.99 really that much cheaper than $20.00? (It's one-twentieth of 1 percent less.) There's even a retailing term for this: it's called "left-digit bias." Walmart has done an excellent job of taking the art of pricing to another level. They commonly set their shelf prices at, for example, $6.87 or $14.73, suggesting that they have shaved even a few more cents off the price.

One brick and mortar retailing concept that is being revived is "clustering." The old thinking was to fear having a competitor right across the street. Then, some brave retailers — mainly auto dealerships — began formal clustering, intentionally grouping competing businesses in the same general area: "auto row." It worked. Informal clustering occurs when similar businesses locate in a concentrated area.

If your online presence is nil or weak, here are some ways to ramp this up. Etsy, eBay, and Amazon all offer e-commerce solutions where you provide the product and they market it for a fee. A second step would be to use Fulfillment by Amazon. With this arrangement, they ship the product from their locations and customers gain some free-shipping options, which are very powerful buying motivators. Of course, your end goal is to have an excellent website as soon as you can. Google "website design" or ask others in business for a recommendation. Don't try this yourself unless it's your field.

And last, a challenge and huge opportunity for retailers: the millennials. Born between 1981 and 2000, much of this generation was raised on high-speed internet, smartphones, digital music devices, and instant messaging. They're massive multitaskers who simultaneously use web-based search, social networking and gaming sites, texting, wikis, and personal blogs.

Wow. Retailing is becoming a whole new ball game. Make sure your team is in the stadium and ready to play.

24 MAKING AN EFFECTIVE PRESENTATION

QUESTION:
I have to make an important business presentation soon and I'm nervous about it. It's imperative that it be smooth and professional. What do I need to know to pull this off?

ANSWER:
There are some basic skills you can learn quickly about making a terrific and convincing business presentation.

Let's talk about this.

We'll look at how you'd prepare for a typical 30 to 60-minute informational-style presentation (that means you, standing at the front of the room). We'll look at the steps to go through, how to prepare and organize your information, some pointers on using visual aids, and several hints for success. To help motivate you, realize that your skills as a good presenter will stay with you throughout your business career and social life.

First, know your audience. This may surprise you: as soon as you have a basic outline of what you're going to talk about, set it aside for a moment. The most important step in preparing your presentation is analyzing the needs of the audience. An otherwise perfect presentation that misses the audience's needs is a flop. As Peter F. Drucker said, "Doing the right thing is more important than doing the thing right." Here are some thoughts to consider:

- Why will the audience be there, and what do they expect?
- What is their knowledge level about my topic?

- Are they greatly above or below me in rank?

- What will motivate them to buy into my idea, product, or service?

Organize your material and yourself. One simple method that's been around for years is to use 3 x 5 note cards. As you research your topic, simply write down ideas, quotations, websites, or other notes — just one per card. Then sort the cards into whatever order produces a good flow of thoughts. This step may take some effort. It's likely that you will, for example: pull some cards out, move cards around within the deck, or insert a new card reading "This needs more research." Once you've decided on an order, number the cards in pencil. Use pencil because in a future presentation you may change the order, remove or add cards, or otherwise change the content.

Now it's time to rehearse. Your objective is to become fluid and not overly dependent on your note cards. If you find yourself flipping through them while you speak (this is very distracting to the audience), consider putting key words on standard size paper. It may be helpful to have a friend or colleague video a few minutes of your practice session and then critique it with you.

If you are informing or persuading, try to stick with three or four main ideas. Set them out with appropriate discussion, facts, and examples. Be sure to review them in your summary and conclusion. If you're asking your audience to take a particular action, be crystal clear about what you want them to do and exactly how to do it.

As you prepare, be aware that your attire, appearance, and demeanor can greatly enhance (or weaken) your presentation.

Use visual aids effectively. These can significantly increase the impact of your presentation and your audience's retention of it. For a small group meeting, the "old school" aids like a flip chart or white board might be appropriate. However, Microsoft PowerPoint is the gold standard for anything bigger. It's fairly easy to learn enough basic skills to create and use an effective PowerPoint visual slideshow. Most community colleges offer both classroom and online instruction on PowerPoint, and of course there are loads of books and other online classes and tutorials available.

Having PowerPoint skills opens up a whole new set of opportunities for your presentation. For example, your notes can be visible to you on the computer screen but not visible to the audience. To add a professional touch, you can use a wireless remote control (around $25), which allows you to control your slides without having to be at the computer. Look for one that has a laser pointer built in. And, in PowerPoint, it's a snap to print handouts, in several different useful formats, for distribution.

Consider these tips from experienced speakers:

- Seek out opportunities to develop your speaking skills, like Toastmasters.
- Visit ahead of time and get comfortable with the room where you will give your presentation.
- Maximize eye contact with the audience. Smile.
- Anticipate obvious questions from your audience and have answers and additional information ready.
- Remember that even if you feel nervous, it's probably not that apparent to others.

In short, the ability to make effective business presentations is a highly valued skill. The basics are easy to learn. Best wishes.

25 WHAT IS "LEAN"?

> ## QUESTION:
> *I'm hearing a lot lately about how some businesses are going "lean." Is this a fad of some kind or a real thing? And what should I know about it?*
>
> ## ANSWER:
> *You certainly need to know about Lean (in this context, it's normally spelled with a capital L). It's here to stay. And, you asked the right guy — I'm a huge Lean proponent.*
>
> *Let's talk about this.*

Lean is definitely not a fad or just the latest cool business technique-of-the-month. It's a whole different way of thinking about how you run your business. Once you get it, you won't go back. In a nutshell, the main principle of Lean is that you make continuous small improvements in your business. The way to do this is by identifying waste and getting rid of it.

We'll talk more about that in a moment. Let's look into the background, general concepts, and benefits of Lean. Then we'll look at some specific techniques and examples. You'll be surprised how easy it is.

The history of Lean manufacturing goes back to Henry Ford in the 1910s. His pioneering use of the assembly line revolutionized how cars were made. It also ushered in some entirely new ways of thinking about mass production. A great deal of modern Lean thinking is based on the Toyota Production System (TPS). As Japan rebuilt its industrial base after World War II, the TPS became established as the successor to mass production. If this interests you, check Wikipedia at "Lean manufacturing" for an excellent historical summary of TPS and Lean. Another good source of general information is the Lean Enterprise Institute, at *lean.org*.

Currently, the principles of Lean are followed in many familiar manufacturing companies. Some Lean names include Toyota, Boeing, GE, Dell, Merck, ALCOA, Honeywell, Porsche, Fluke, and Heath Techna. Notice that these companies are leaders in their industries.

In the 100-plus years since Ford's first assembly line, the Lean concept has evolved and expanded from manufacturing into many other fields of business. Lean thinking has been pulled into health care (Virginia Mason Hospital); transportation (Southwest Airlines); fast food (Subway); and even government (U.S. Department of Defense, State of Minnesota). As managers see the benefits of operating Lean, another wave now finds Lean business practices in all sorts of small and service businesses, and even in personal lives.

Here is a central point of Lean thinking: to eliminate waste, you first have to be able to recognize and identify it. Waste is anything that does not add value to your products and services. So then the question becomes, what is value? Value is anything your customers or clients will pay for. So the conclusion is that waste is anything your customers are not willing to pay extra for. Your goal in going Lean is to identify and eliminate these non-value-adding activities. This is called "mapping the value stream."

Lean is not a marketing campaign plan or a short-term cost reduction program. It's a fundamental way a whole company operates. It has to become the culture of your company. The phrase "Lean transformation" is often used to describe how a company converts from an older way of thinking. In brief, a Lean business focuses on continuous improvement by identifying waste and eliminating it. It's an incremental process that can start small and then notch forward. It takes commitment from everybody. And it's fun!

Here's a quick overview of some examples of waste:

Overproduction. This is the making of whatever your end product is (e.g., finished products, architectural drawings, financial planning documents, floral arrangements) in greater amounts or complexity than is actually valued by your client.

Transportation. Your customers pay only for value-added processes — they don't pay anyone to move parts around from one production line to another, or documents from one office to another. Some transportation is, of course, necessary, but it should be minimized.

Waiting and idle time. Waste occurs when employees can't perform value-added work because they have to wait for incoming information or materials, or when they are tied to a workflow process that has excessive wait time built into it.

Excess motion. Work processes should be designed so that employees don't have to reach or walk around to get the supplies, tools, or data that they need. Unnecessary motion adds no value.

Rework. This expensive waste occurs when any work product (goods or services) has to be redone or repaired due to errors or defects. The best thinking on this is simple: minimize your "fix-it factory."

Intellectual underuse. This waste refers to the missed opportunity of using your employees' skills to their fullest. It's an invisible waste because you won't know about it unless you ask.

But one caution here: not every business is a candidate for Lean implementation. If it is done for the wrong reasons or improperly, or if some employees resist change and would be holdouts (anchor draggers), you would definitely have problems. Get good advice before you commit.

Some sources for more information:

- Visit *lean.org* for loads of good ideas and links.

- Go to the FastCap website (*fastcap.com*) and select "Lean Videos" from the "Videos" tab. Excellent and concise information.

- The *Complete Idiot's Guide, For Dummies*, and *Demystified* book series (such as *"Business Math Demystified"* by Allan Bluman) all have good offerings on Lean. Check the library around call number 658.

- Search Google for "lean business principles" and see what fits your interests.

- Five names to Google for blogs and other information: Mark Graban, James Womack, Jay Arthur, Jeffrey Liker, Eric Ries.

Other things being equal, a Lean operation has a significant competitive advantage. After a Lean transformation, a business will typically have increased sales, higher margins, and lower expenses. What's not to like?

And next time you're in a Subway, watch the value-added production of your sandwich, from order to checkout.

26 WHAT IS MY EXIT STRATEGY?

QUESTION:
I was asked recently about my "exit strategy" for my small business. I hadn't heard of this, so I just said that I wasn't really sure yet. What do I need to know?

ANSWER:
An exit strategy is a very important component of your business planning. Any time you start something, you need to think about how it might end. You have loads of choices.

Let's talk about this.

First, a caveat: this discussion assumes that your business is doing OK. To be clear, an exit strategy is not a rescue mission. It's your plan for how you will maximize your gain and success from the business over time.

Many people find that the basic "countdown method" works fine. Here's how it might go: say you plan to exit by selling the business in five years. The first year (five years left), focus on gaining customers and building sales volume. With four years left, experiment; try some new products, services, or markets. At three years left, evaluate what's working and ditch some of the less successful moves. Two years out, focus on your most profitable products, services, and markets. Also, dial back a bit on any discretionary expenses. During the final year, limit your marketing budget and spend it only on proven sales generators. Slash nonessential expenses, and clear out any old inventory. This will yield great financial statements to show prospective buyers.

Here are ten examples of exit strategies, with more information and thoughts:

1. **Sell outright, as a going concern.** Your business is humming, so find a buyer and negotiate the price and terms. There are two basic ways to proceed: as a sale of all or some of the business assets; or as a sale of the whole business entity, such as an LLC. It's cleaner for you to sell the entity but typically, the buyer would prefer the asset sale. This is largely because the buyer, in taking the entity as a whole, gets all the liabilities too — including those that are hidden or unknown.

2. **Hand down to the next generation.** Warning! Start early, because it will take time to train the new owners and bring them fully in. It's essential that you have a written succession and transition plan and that all parties use it as a guide.

3. **Sell to employees.** One or more of your staff may be interested, especially if you agree to stay on (typically with compensation) as a spokesperson and advisor for a time.

4. **Be acquired.** A competitor or other company may want your products, services, or markets. In larger firms, this is often done with a mix of cash and a stock swap.

5. **Sell to a supplier or a customer.** This practice, called vertical integration, is advantageous to the buyer because it gives them an additional profit margin and, of course, control over their new holding.

6. **Sell your share to your existing partners.** This strategy is common among professional practices. A written succession plan or other buyout document is a must.

7. **Bring in a partner.** If you own the business alone, you might have a partner for a preset period and then sell your share to your partner. Be sure you have a written partnership agreement spelling out each partner's rights and duties and detailing the timeline for the buyout. It is common for a selling partner to provide financing for the purchase. Be very careful whom you ally with.

8. **Go public.** Occasionally a small business will grow large enough to offer its stock to the public. This involves a great deal of specialized legal work with securities laws and regulations; fees can easily top $100,000. If this is your strategy, get high-powered legal and accounting help from day one.

9. **Schedule a timed endpoint.** Some business owners plan to operate a business for a set period and then shut it down and move on to greener pastures. When that time comes, the owner sells the assets and closes the company. One strategy that fits with this is to lease any needed property and equipment, setting up the leases so they all end at the same time. Poof.

10. **Milk it.** Here's a relatively recent non-exit strategy: it's called running a "lifestyle business." In this model, a skilled owner/ manager builds the business up to the point where employees are doing most or all of the work. The owner's role is minimal because the business is stable and profitable. If someone asked, "Why don't you sell your business?" your answer might be "Why would I? It's an easy part-time job, at $8,000 a month."

Google "business exit strategy" for loads more on this. As Steven Covey says in *The 7 Habits of Highly Effective People*, "Begin with the end in mind." As you can see, a little up-front planning for your exit can help you make better decisions all along the way.

27 WHAT IS A "SMALL" BUSINESS?

QUESTION:

I'm confused about the definition of a "small business." When I read business magazines like Forbes *or see online articles at* Inc. *magazine's website, they talk about things like your board of directors, or your accounting staff, or other topics that have nothing to do with me. I can't identify with this, because I run an* **actual** *small business. What's the deal?*

ANSWER:

You are right — most of those national media lean toward using "small business" at a scale that we are not familiar with. This is partly because it's popular to include any possible mention of small business.

Let's talk about this.

Here's the scoop. A big part of the problem is that the SBA has set pretty broad standards for what qualifies as a small business. A main criterion is that the business is not dominant in its field. After that, the size of the business is generally measured by either sales revenue or number of employees. It may surprise you to find out that a business with hundreds of employees and millions in sales might be included. That's probably not most people's definition of a small business. The SBA's Office of Advocacy says that about 97 percent of all U.S. businesses are classified as small.

Running a small business is not just a miniature version of chairing a big business. It's qualitatively different. Nearly every business with 100 or more employees will have several departments and some middle managers. The CEO's role is to lead and coordinate the departments. But in a smaller operation, you wear many hats and are much closer to the front end — your customers and clients.

For topics and information tailored to small businesses, check out *Entrepreneur* magazine's excellent website, *entrepreneur.com*. In addition to current topics and articles, they offer a searchable archive of past business articles. Most of this information is relevant to what we think of as actual small businesses.

Another source of current and relevant information is the trade associations. You may not realize that many other people in your same business, nationally and internationally, share ideas and information. You need to get in on this. Nearly every field of business has trade groups with newsletters, blogs, and other current information. You can easily find these online. For example, the owner of a floral shop would Google "trade association florists" to see what's available. Scroll down through the first several pages and pick out what might be useful.

Trade groups may give you new ideas about how to run your business. Also, there are most likely trade magazines available to you at little or no cost. Many now ask for a small "postage offset" of $10 or $15 a year. The reason they're free to you is that they sell your eyeballs to their advertisers.

Closer to home, consider joining the local chamber of commerce or similar organization. Keep up with the business scene through the local newspaper and other newspapers and their websites. A local magazine might focus on small business companies and topics. Plus, SCORE and the Small Business Development Center are available to meet in person, free, and confidentially.

By the way, the longstanding correlation between a company's total sales, employee count, and market value is changing. Consider this: one small business, Instagram, was a young company — less than two years old. It had just thirteen employees when Facebook bought it for $1 billion. Was this really a small business?

Here are three websites with valuable small business content:

- *Bloomberg Businessweek* online (they recently merged), at *bloomberg.com/businessweek*

- My Business (from Australia), at *mybusiness.com.au*

- Small Business Trends (for news and brief articles), at *smallbiztrends.com*

You should know a little bit about the North American Industry Classification System, or NAICS. This is pronounced "nakes." The SBA uses NAICS to establish eligibility for loans and set-asides for government contracts. As the name suggests, it was developed jointly by the United States, Canada, and Mexico. A six-digit code number is assigned depending on how your business is defined. You can find your NAICS code at *naics.com*.

Two surprising but typical examples: in footwear manufacturing, a small business is one with fewer than 1,000 employees. In electronics stores, a small business is one with sales under $30 million annually.

So it looks like the term "small business" is pretty much in the eye of the beholder.

28 SHOULD MY BUSINESS BE "GREEN"?

QUESTION:
I keep hearing that many small businesses are "going green." It seems like this has been around a while now. So, is it more than a fad? What do I need to know about this and is my business a candidate? I guess I'm pretty "green" about going green.

ANSWER:
To some extent, every business is a candidate to go green. Small businesses have been leaders in what many call the green revolution.

Let's talk about this.

First, here's the backstory. The environmental movement had its origins in the 1960s and 1970s, bringing significant change and social awareness of concepts like conservation and environmental concern. In 1973, a shortage of gasoline led to rationing and long lines at the pumps. This helped the nation realize that resources are not limitless. The celebration of Earth Day on April 22 also began in the 1970s. Earth Day falls near the older Arbor Day holiday, dating back to the Teddy Roosevelt presidency in 1907, when every American was expected to plant a tree.

Now, let's look into some green-speak. These are terms and ideas that you'll need to know about to be a player in the world of green business. Here is a glossary of twelve key terms that are common in green discussion circles:

Benefit corporation, or B corporation. This refers to a company that is driven by societal goals in addition to shareholder needs. It is not a legally designated corporate structure, but the business must be certified and agree to a set of specific reporting requirements.

Corporate social responsibility. This concept, often referred to as CSR, is related to what's called the triple bottom line. The term is often used interchangeably with corporate responsibility or corporate citizenship. It envisions a type of corporate self-regulation that accounts for the environmental and social impacts of operations along with financial performance.

Dow Jones Sustainability Index (DJSI). Created in 1999, this is the first global stock index that assesses the financial performance of companies that emphasize sustainability. It has been controversial. Most people haven't heard of it, but it is used as a badge of corporate greening by the rated recipients. Google "DJSI" for more on this.

Downcycling. This is the process of recycling in such a way that new products are of considerably lesser quality or economic value. An example would be clean white paper downcycled into cardboard.

E-waste. This is waste associated with outdated electronic equipment; also called "technotrash."

Green supply chain management. A supply chain is the steps through which a company sources, designs, manufacturers, and delivers its products to customers. So "greening the supply chain" is an effort to reduce the environmental impact of each stage in the production cycle of a product. This is from the sourcing of the raw materials used to construct it, to its distribution and sale, and finally to its potential to be recycled, reused, or composted.

Greenwashing. This derogatory term, derived from "whitewashing," refers to how an organization, product, or service is represented as being green or environmentally sustainable when it actually isn't.

Leadership in Energy and Environmental Design (LEED). The LEED building rating system was developed by the U.S. Green Building Council and launched in 1998. It is internationally recognized and provides certification standards for environmentally sustainable construction. The standards take into account energy and water efficiency, carbon dioxide emissions reduction, improved indoor environmental quality, and responsible raw material sourcing.

Life cycle impact assessment. This refers to a compilation and evaluation of the inputs, outputs, and potential environmental impacts of a product or system throughout its life span. Environmental burdens include the materials and energy resources required to create the product, as well as the wastes and emissions generated during the process. It is similar to a financial analysis of the life cycle cost of an item.

Repurposing. This describes a product being cleaned or refurbished and then reused in its previous form, or in a new form, thereby extending its useful life. For fun, Google "trash talk-news from the dumpster" for great innovative examples of creative reuse.

Triple bottom line. A company or organization's set of values used to track their financial, social, and environmental performance as a way to measure success.

Upcycling. A process of recycling that yields new products of higher economic value. Example: using waste plastic from soda bottles (PET) to create TerraTex fabric or Trex composite decking.

There's tons of "greening" information on the internet. For a good overview, start at *greenbiz.com*.

29 GENERATIONS IN THE WORKPLACE

QUESTION:

I used to be pretty good at dealing with people, but now it seems like people have become completely unpredictable. What's going on? Am I missing something?

ANSWER:

There are some good reasons for your confusion. Here's the deal: These days, we have four very distinct generations of folks in the workplace. Each generation has its own different values, experiences, outlook, and technology. Workplace conflict is becoming a very real concern.

Let's talk about this.

First off, realize that we're talking about everybody. That's your clients and customers, your employees, your suppliers, and pretty much anyone whom you interact with in business. (And don't forget your family and other relationships too.)

The social fabric of America is always changing. But never before have we had such distinct generational groups. Each cohort has tens of millions of people who share their similar group values. You need to be aware of how this affects the workplace.

Consider this: if you have little in common with someone, have very different values, don't really speak the same language, and don't identify or empathize with them — well, that's not exactly a recipe for success, is it?

Having a better understanding of these generational traits and differences will help you in dealing with those around you.

Let's review some common characteristics of these four groups. This discussion will involve some broad stereotypes about people. As with all generalizations, obviously not every observation applies to every member of any group.

The traditionalists. This group, also referred to as the Silent Generation, includes those born between 1928-1945. These folks are now in their mid-70s and older. Around 95 percent have retired. Those who remain in the workforce are generally very high-status. They may be members of corporate boards, emeritus professors, prominent elected officials, or senior partners in professional firms.

These are high-knowledge people who created much of the business structure and culture we have today. Many of them worked for just one employer for their entire career, a concept now considered quaint. Their parents lived through the Great Depression.

To help understand them, here are some typical characteristics:

- Frugal and fiscally conservative
- Rule-oriented; work within the system
- Simple in lifestyle
- Loyal to company and others

The baby boomers. Born from 1946–1964, this large group of Americans has had a profound effect on American life and culture. Today, they're 58–76 years old. Every day, 10,000 more boomers turn 65. This will continue for about ten years.

The boomers grew up during the post-World War II American heyday. They, with their parents, lived through many major events and changes in American history. Examples: the Civil Rights era, the moon landing, Vietnam, the Hippie era, the Cold War, computerization. They are family-oriented and love their culture, music, books, and friends.

This age cohort has ruled the workplace for decades. They are very focused. Until recently, the boomers were the largest population group, at about 76 million.

Typical workplace characteristics:

- Comfortable with who they are
- Very career-oriented
- Apprehensive about retirement
- Work hard and deliver the goods

Generation X (Gen X). This smaller group of 45 million folks, born from 1965 to around 1980, brings a somewhat different view to the workplace. They're now in their 40s and 50s, in mid career. Some formative events as they grew up: Three Mile Island meltdown, 9/11, multiple recessions, minivans, "latchkey kids", parental divorce, AIDS awareness. Like the boomers, Gen Xers are planners and schedulers.

Typical workplace characteristics:

- View career as a lattice, not an ascending ladder
- Afraid of being wedged in between the 150-plus million Boomers and millennials
- Very computer- and tech-empowered
- Independent and self-reliant

The millennials (or Generation Y). Well, stand back — it's a whole new ball game. This immense group — 80-plus million in number — is a big departure from their predecessors. Born from 1981–2000, they are now in their 20s to early 40s. They have grown up with unprecedented levels of technology. They enjoy immediate, constant communication. Some life-shaping events for these folks: the 9/11 terrorist attacks, dissolution of the USSR, the internet, Facebook, enormous technological advances, globalization, the social media explosion, smartphones, a flood of tech devices.

The millennial generation is often judged self-absorbed and narcissistic. A cover story in *Time* magazine called the millennials "the ME ME ME generation … lazy … fame-obsessed … attention sponges." Human resources professionals joke that millennials are addicted to winning "participation trophies." The general perception of millennials is that they are self-absorbed slackers, stunted in emotional growth, and full of entitlement.

Sorry for trashing them, but this perception is supported by numerous studies. A recent Clark University (Worcester, Mass.) "Poll of Emerging Adults" found that more millennials ages 18–29 live with their parents than with a spouse. A high school commencement speech titled "You Are Not Special" drew attention to this perception of entitlement. Check out the 12-minute video on YouTube.

While all of that may be true, here's the takeaway point: the enormous millennial generation will certainly inherit, and hopefully solve, the problems and challenges we face today. Fast-forward mentally to 2040. All the boomers are gone from the workforce. The relatively few Gen Xers are now 60 to 75 and of little and descending influence. The 80 million millennials are in their prime workplace years (40–60) and are ascending in power.

Unlike their predecessor generations, millennials tend to be collaborators and very fluid team players. In the workplace, they exhibit these characteristics:

- Enjoy constant multitasking
- Want detailed and immediate feedback on job performance
- Work well in groups
- Are optimistic — "There must be an app for that"
- Prefer informal attire — every day should be like casual Friday
- Expect a more relaxed work-life balance

Let's look at three examples of ways the millennials depart from their predecessors. These differences will increasingly manifest themselves in workplace relations in future years.

Ethnic diversity. The millennials are by far the most racially and ethnically diverse generation in American history. According to recent data from the Pew Research Center, this cohort is about 19 percent Hispanic; 14 percent Black; 4 percent Asian; 4 percent mixed race or other; and 60 percent white, which is a record low. You need to be sure that your business policies and dealings clearly recognize this diversity.

Body artwork. Older generations have an entirely different view of, for example, large, obvious tattoos. To older folks, these are a form of rebellion. Same with skin piercings and prominent metalwear. But to many younger GenXers and most millennials, "tats" and metal are viewed as positive self-expression and as attractive body adornments.

Interpersonal communication. The millennials thrive on constant and instant communication. In the workplace, this means frequent feedback and direction. Forget about the old annual performance review idea. That concept would be a joke with millennials whose timeline for responses is measured in hours or minutes.

So this is clear: the millennial takeover of American society, and of the business scene, is now underway. If you are still not convinced of the magnitude of this impending change, consider this: there are now numerous major human resources and other consulting firms specializing in how to help companies adapt to the upcoming onslaught of the millennials. According to a recent *Forbes* article, "91% of millennials aspire to leadership." Google "Why Millennials Want To Be Leaders In The Workplace Now More Than Ever" to check this out.

30 TIME MANAGEMENT

> **QUESTION:**
> *In my business, it seems like there's always much more to do than there is time available to do it. My schedule overflows even when I try to keep it on track. Are there some ways to get my time under control?*
>
> **ANSWER:**
> *Yes, and your problem is very common. Sounds like you could use some time management advice.*
>
> *Let's talk about this.*

First off, we need to clear up one major thing: time management is not about your management of time. It's about your management of yourself. Everyone has the same 24 hours in a day; it's all about how you use them. There always are, and always will be, more things to do than there is time to do them.

Let's look at some self-management ideas.

Spend some time planning and organizing. A formula that works for many is to devote about 10 percent of your day to planning and prioritizing. A written planning method like a daily/hourly scheduling system is OK, but be aware that digital methods like using a PDA or smartphone are much more useful and flexible.

Organize in a way that works for you. For some, that means file piles, where tasks are visible on your desk. For some, it's a to-do list, with a priority number or ranking like 1–5 for each item. Others find a whiteboard or project management software to be more effective. Consider using a simple color code for importance or priority — for example, a red highlighted task takes precedence.

Distinguish between what's urgent and what's important. The word urgent implies that you must attend to something right now. But what urgent really means is just that something must be dealt with right now, if at all. Urgent activities usually have high visibility. Common example: your phone rings; you must decide within a few seconds whether to answer it. It may be an important call, or it may not. On the other hand, important matters have lasting impact. A planned and important task should override lesser priorities, even if they seem urgent at the moment. Allocate your time to your important priorities. Don't let an unimportant issue of the moment drive you off task.

Leverage your time. As your business grows, add people who can work without heavy supervision. Use delegation to amplify your effectiveness. Is this task something that really needs your continuing involvement, or can someone else take this on? If you keep doing all the important things yourself, how will your staff develop the skills needed to handle projects and problems on their own?

Learn how to say no. If you're maxed out, be very guarded about taking on an additional task. Taking it on could mean you would have to do it poorly, cut into time for an existing high priority, or both. It may be gratifying to think that you're the go-to person, but if heading up that local charity fundraiser during your busiest time of the year just doesn't fit, better say so. Rehearse a tactful turndown, something like, "It's flattering that you asked, and I'd love to lend a hand, but could we talk about some ways I could help out during my off-season?"

Realize that your employees may be in the same situation. If you approach an employee with a task assignment, it's perfectly appropriate for that person to ask you for help with prioritizing how the new task fits in with his or her current workload.

Use your peak time to advantage. Most people have a time of day when they're most alert and productive. Use yours for the toughest tasks.

Ask yourself "Lakein's question." This term is a reference to a classic 1973 time management book. Frequently think, "What is the best use of my time right now?" This is very helpful when you find an unexpected bit of time — for example, a last-minute appointment cancellation.

Each week, identify a time waster and get rid of it. For example, if you usually sit in on a low-payoff meeting, stop going. Or, look at your bulging email inbox — it may be time to unsubscribe from some of the senders of low-value messages. If your job involves lots of paperwork, try to handle each item as few times as possible. Every time you pick up an item, move it along to the next stage rather than just putting it back on the pile.

For more ideas, Google "business time management tips" and see what might suit your needs and situation. Keep in mind that time is the ultimate perishable. When it's gone … it's gone.

STAGE FOUR:
MATURITY

Be aware of new opportunities as they arise. Carefully monitor your Key Performance Indicators. Are you still on target? If not, what needs to happen, and how will you fix this? Plan on working this stage to the max. The longer it is, the better, as it provides your highest profit accumulation.

Introductory Thoughts

- Don't overlook using press releases as a marketing tool. You have something of value to communicate.

- Take every opportunity to improve your personal business skills.

- Look ahead to what's coming in the next stage, renewal or decline — are you ready to take action?

- Be aware that your management ability and style need to evolve as your business grows.

- Evaluate any new or innovative products or services that may be an opportunity. This is a good time to experiment.

- How you manage your business's maturity stage will determine how long it lasts — months or years.

31 WHY DO PEOPLE BUY?

QUESTION:
My small business is doing OK but not growing much. I think it would help if I knew more about what motivates people to buy a particular product or service. Why do people buy? What's the scoop?

ANSWER:
There's some history here, and some recent research on "buyology." You may or may not like where it's going.

Let's talk about this.

Here's a fun metaphor to start our discussion. Look at it this way: all of your prospective customers or clients are avid listeners of these two major radio stations: WII-FM, and MMFG-AM. The joke is that WII-FM stands for "What's In It-For Me," and MMFG-AM is "Make Me Feel Good-About Myself." A great deal of the purchase decision is driven by emotional needs — for example, to feel important, fulfilled, attractive, or successful.

The "why people buy" question has been around quite a while. In 1957, journalist Vance Packard released a book called *The Hidden Persuaders*. Although it was primarily about business and marketing, it also reflected on the 1956 U.S. presidential election, when, for the first time, television ads were the dominant medium for both sides. Here's some perspective: back then, there were only three primary broadcast channels, reception was via an ugly metal antenna on the roof, and the typical TV had a grainy, low-res, 18-inch black-and-white screen.

Packard's main point was that sinister and manipulative techniques like subliminal advertising were being brought into the marketplace. In his view, these controlling tricks were driving and distorting how people made buying decisions. He was partly right. That was the beginning of an explosive 30 years of growth in how we were marketed to by a flood of skilled and targeted advertising pitches. Later, during the golden age of television, an ad during a top-rated show on one of the Big Three networks could reach 70 percent of the viewing audience.

A major marketing research firm, Yankelovich, recently estimated that today, a person living in a typical American city is exposed to 5,000 advertising messages daily. We're all in sensory overload from every direction. Some examples: ads printed on tray tables in planes, floods of pop-up ads in websites, logo-heavy reusable shopping bags, and an avalanche of product placement exposures in television shows and movies. Fans of the long-running show *Hawaii Five-O* may wonder if it's an action show or a Chevrolet advertisement.

If you're in small business, you're on both sides of this issue. It's important that you know how to effectively address your target customers and you also need to be aware that as a consumer, you make buying decisions yourself, too.

Theories abound about exactly how people make the decision to buy something. Most of these theories make a distinction between buying necessities (staple foods, basic clothing, laundry soap) and other less-necessary or discretionary buying decisions (dinner out, upscale jewelry, artwork). Here are some dimensions and ideas about why people buy.

Price. The price of an item or service is important to nearly all buyers. Interesting situation: a few years ago, JCPenney tested out a new pricing strategy called "Fair and Square." Merchandise was marked at a "low everyday" price. It did not work well, and sales fell dramatically. Price-oriented customers don't feel like they're getting a deal unless something is on sale. We're all conditioned to respond to those prominent "30% off" signs.

Status and image. Many purchases are made with a prod from the ego: flashy cars, high-end wristwatches, country club memberships. Also, consider a lifestyle item like a hybrid car or a Tesla, where a big component of the purchase is "what it says about me."

Convenience. Many goods and services are purchased because they offer high ease of use. Examples: a refrigerator icemaker or a weekly lawn-mowing service.

Loyalty. Certain purchases have a very high brand loyalty element. Examples: Apple products, soft drinks, or cosmetics.

Enjoyment, pleasure, or entertainment. Most people buy, at least occasionally, something simply for fun. This could be a product like sports equipment, a spa visit, or tickets to a concert.

As with all else in business, things are constantly changing. Two books make this very clear. In *Buyology*, author Martin Lindstrom reports his findings after a three-year, $7 million "neuromarketing" study of consumer brain function that involved brain scans (functional MRIs) of 2,000 people. Check chapter summaries at *martinlindstrom.com*.

In *Why We Buy*, Paco Underhill discusses his company's fascinating analyses of consumer behaviors under various conditions. The subtitle *The Science of Shopping* is accurate. For further thoughts, Google "book reviews why we buy."

In the final analysis, why people buy may be as complex and unknowable as why people fall in love.

32 MEDIA RELEASE BASICS

QUESTION:
My small business has an anniversary coming up, plus some other recent developments that I'd like to point out to the community, but I don't really have any PR skills or training. How can I get the word out?

ANSWER:
Media releases are an excellent way to get your announcement, accomplishment, or special event out to folks. And even better, it's free!

Let's talk about this.

First, sooner or later most every business will have something worthy of putting out to the public. For example, a first anniversary in business warrants a brief media release. This may surprise you: even a small city may have 20 or more active media outlets. Of course, some are quite large and some very small and specialized. Your local chamber of commerce will have a list of media and their contact info.

Second, you'll need to follow some guidelines to improve your chances of getting exposure. You need to think like a reporter or editor. At the very least, make it easy for them to run your media release without having to do lots of rework on it. Another objective is to get them to contact you for a follow-up discussion. Here are the basic things to know for a fairly informal local press or broadcast media release:

Use standard formatting for your media release. There's a basic layout to follow. For your release to look professional and attract interest, you'll need to include certain information, in an expected order:

- Use a common font and point size, like 12 point Arial, and double space the lines; one-page limit.

- Top of page should show company letterhead and basic information.

- Put the words "PRESS RELEASE" in all caps.

- Supply a contact person's name, phone number, and email address. The media may reach out for more information, which is good.

- State "FOR IMMEDIATE RELEASE" (or a later release date if the media has agreed to an embargo).

- You might suggest a title — be sure to include an action verb — but realize this is the editor's prerogative.

Put the news up on top. Your important information should be in the first paragraph and should contain a "hook" to secure the interest of editors and, hopefully, readers or listeners. The contents should be an inverted pyramid, with the most important items appearing first. Then each succeeding paragraph should contain less important points and more details. Consider this: if just the first half of your 400-word release gets printed, are all your main points still intact?

Lay out some concrete facts. Examples of some good topics: a new product or service, adding employees, landing a major contract, or a notable milestone or achievement.

Use plain business English. Press releases should be written in plain business language. Keep explanations simple. If you have a complex sentence with more than one idea, the next sentence should be just a few words. Use layman's terms; avoid overly technical language and insider jargon. Use numbers sparingly.

Be aware of media rules for grammar and punctuation. These are a bit different from those in normal correspondence. For example, in newspaper copy, there is only one space between sentences. Also spell out most abbreviations and acronyms upon first use. For example, at first reference: Whatcom Community College; after that, WCC would be OK. For most media, the authority for this is the *Associated Press Stylebook*. Check at your local library reference desk, or you can buy a copy for about $25. For a free, concise summary, Google "AP Stylebook summary" and choose what looks good.

Focus on facts. Ditch superlatives like "best" or "cheapest." Make simple declarative statements about who, what, when, where, why, and how. Focus on something that has happened or is going to happen. Avoid fluff: this is a news release, not an advertisement.

Adjust the release for broadcast media. The guidelines for broadcast media are a bit different. The same release will be much shorter, unless it's a really major event. Figure on about three spoken words per second. So if you think the station may give your release thirty seconds of air, that's only ninety words. Be sure you have a designated spokesperson with a sound bite script ready in case the station calls. Try to include a bit of new information in the script that isn't in the release. Don't be too nervous about this; if you falter or flub, they can edit it or not use it at all.

Submit it electronically. Send your release to a media outlet's newsroom by email. Check their website for a specific person who covers business topics and direct it to him or her.

In summary, consider how media releases can become an important part of your marketing and communications strategy. Get help if you need it. Google "sample press release" for dozens of examples. For more information and suggestions, check out *wikihow.com/Write-a-Press-Release*.

33 HAVING EMPLOYEES IS A REAL CHALLENGE. ANY HINTS?!

QUESTION:
I now have employees to supervise and I'm very uneasy about two things: doing their annual performance reviews, and how to fire someone if I need to. Can you help me dial down the apprehension meter a bit on these two concerns?

ANSWER:
These are very common fears for a new employer or supervisor. And clearly your actions in this area can help or harm your company. Some basic skills are easy to learn.

Let's talk about this.

The annual **performance review** or evaluation became built in to the American business scene decades ago. Back then, it was the basis for pay, promotion, and career decisions. It's still very formalized in many governmental agencies and highly layered corporations. It's generally known that both supervisors and employees detest the process. It's an old model, but realize that some people still have that mindset.

The new model is very different. First off, ditch the annual idea. Today's business environment changes much too quickly to wait a year for just about anything. The trend is clearly toward much more frequent feedback, perhaps monthly or even weekly. Leadership has become more of an ongoing process, like coaching. In fact, many small businesses where most or all of the employees work in one building or area hold a brief all-staff meeting at the start of each day. Of course, this is not like an employee review, but it shows the value of continuous feedback and having everyone on the same page. If you're thinking of making your business a Lean company, keep this in mind.

To conduct a successful review, you need a suitable setting. It has to be comfortable and private (so, not the coffee shop across the street). Don't allow interruptions from others. Allow ample time for discussion. As a rule of thumb, try to do one-third talking and two-thirds listening.

You'll need an employee evaluation form, checklist, or similar document. These forms typically have three parts: a description of a task or attribute, a rating scale (often in numbers like 1–10 or words like excellent, good, average, fair, poor), and a comments and discussion section. Google "employee assessment form" and find one that suits your needs. Ask other managers for suggestions. It's best to use the same form for all employees at the same level.

Here are some suggestions to prepare for a successful evaluation session:

- To gain confidence, try some role-playing with a creative friend or colleague. Be sure to play both roles. Gain some experience using your evaluation form.

- Before the meeting, review the job description for the position. This is a good time to consider whether revisions are necessary and should be discussed.

- It's very common now to have the employee fill out a brief self-assessment and bring it to the meeting.

- Nothing you say in the review should come as a surprise to the employee. This is not the time for a "gotcha" but rather for a collaborative approach. If you have a serious criticism, be specific and constructive.

- Fill out the evaluation form in plain view of the employee. Consider sitting at a table (side by side, or adjacent sides) instead of across a desk.

- End the review on a supportive note.

As to **firing**, here are the bare basics you should know. Employment law is very complex. Most states are employment at-will states. This means that both the employer and employee are free to end the employment relationship at any time, absent an agreement to the contrary. There are exceptions to at-will, but generally you can terminate an employee at any time for any legal reason, or give no reason. Examples of illegal reasons: gender, age, race, physical disability, or sexual orientation.

Let's assume you've done all you can to get the employee on track. Now it's time to part ways in the least destructive manner. Some hints:

- Come directly to the point. "John, I'm sure this is no surprise to you. I have to let you go."

- Be prepared for a "Why?" question. Here's one answer: "Well, we've talked about specifics before. There's no future for you here."

- If asked for just one more chance: "I'm sorry, the decision's been made. You're better off moving on now rather than later."

- Offer the employee a choice: the person can clean out his or her workspace, or you will box up the belongings and send them.

- Be security aware. An angry firee may feel vindictive. Be sure to get any keys and reset applicable passwords.

- And last, the instant you sense any possible legal tangles, talk with an experienced attorney.

34 HOW CAN I INCREASE THE VALUE OF MY BUSINESS?

QUESTION:
I often wonder about how the value (sales price) of a small business is determined. This leads me to ask: What are some things I can do to make my business more valuable?

ANSWER:
If your goal is to eventually sell your business, it's best to start with that idea in mind from day one. If you didn't do this, you need to shift your thinking pronto. You'll need to show several years of successful performance to support your asking price.

Let's talk about this.

The value or asking price of a business is a subjective opinion that is usually based on three approaches: reviewing the business's assets, analyzing its cash flow, and researching sales of other comparable businesses. Usually, the most important factor is determining what's called the "seller's discretionary cash flow." A potential purchaser is very interested in buying a stream of income, above and among other things.

Think of Aesop's fable about the goose that lays golden eggs. What is the goose worth? It depends on how many eggs the goose lays and how long it lays them. Your business is viewed the same way. What cash stream will the business dependably produce, and for how long?

Here are five ways to boost the value of your business:

Be ready with organized, professional financial statements and projections. No savvy buyer is interested in a pig in a poke. The buyer and likely some outside professionals will be performing due diligence, which means that they will be looking intently at your financials and your operation as a whole. In the year or two presale, work to increase revenues and contain expenses.

Part of the financial scrutiny will involve what accountants call "ratio analysis." Depending on the size of your business, your balance sheet and income statement may get a real going-over. Examples of typical subjects for analysis: profit margins, inventory turnover, and expense ratios. If this topic interests you, Google it or go to the reference desk at your library and ask about "Risk Management Association annual statement studies."

A quality sales brochure would be helpful. If you're considering using a business broker to assist your sale, their office will do much of this work. In return, you'll owe a commission (maybe 10 percent) if they bring you an acceptable buyer.

Make yourself less essential to the business. Your buyer must be able to visualize him- or herself running the business. Your strategy is to build your business with quality employees who know their jobs. A prospective buyer would expect an organizational chart and a set of job descriptions. The business sale process should never be a surprise to anyone.

If you are important to the operation of the business — for example, a key part of its production or branding — then you may have to offer to stay on for an agreed period of time, say as a producer or a spokesperson. You can expect some compensation for this; the buyer gets an expense deduction for your fee.

Work on your relationships. A business that is known throughout the community for civic-mindedness will command a premium. Also realize that a serious buyer will want to talk with your major clients, customers, and suppliers about their intent to continue doing business with the company.

Offer attractive terms and conditions. It's pretty uncommon for a buyer to pay cash up front for the asking price. You should be clear that you're open to offers that include your carrying a note for part of the purchase price. Also consider that if your business has some large assets, like real estate or substantial equipment, you could retain ownership of those and lease them to the buyer. This can work well for both buyer and seller.

Another idea is to offer an earnout. This is a deal structure where the sale price of the business is adjusted up or down based on the actual performance of the business after the sale. But caution! Be very careful if you're taking the risk and the buyer has little to lose.

Have valuable intellectual property (IP) to include. Second only to having a strong net income stream, value is raised greatly by including some unique and legally protected IP. This could include trademarks, copyrights, patents, and service marks. The last can be as simple as made-up words for a special service you offer, and they may get protection with the symbol ^{SM}. IP provides a basis for goodwill, which means that your business has additional value above and beyond its net earnings. For lots of info on this topic, go to *uspto.gov*.

If selling your business is your goal, start planning right away.

35 TEAM BUILDING IN BUSINESS

QUESTION:
The more employees I add, the less it seems like we're all working together as a group. What can I do to get us all back together?

ANSWER:
It's pretty common for a growing small business to need refocusing. Sounds like your group is ready for some team building activities.

Let's talk about this.

We'll first look into the concept and history of team building in a business setting. Then we'll go over some general thoughts on designing activities. Next, we'll look at an example activity, followed by some sources of information.

A team building activity, also called a group development exercise, is an inexpensive and fun way to get your group back on track. One simple definition of a team is a group of interacting individuals sharing a common goal, plus the responsibility for achieving it. Problems frequently arise when those goals and responsibilities are shared by employees who have little contact. For example, a front-end employee (salesperson) and a back-office worker (bookkeeper) may have very little direct interaction. And as you noted, new hires need help integrating in. Another good time for a group exercise is if you've had several employee positions turn over recently.

If you need any further incentive, realize that workplace friction is expensive. A happy and harmonious workgroup is much more creative and productive.

A simple activity might be a 15-minute exercise during a regular weekly meeting. At the far extreme is an elaborate all-day retreat at a swanky secluded location with catered food and a professional facilitator. This is expensive and requires shutting down the company for the day.

Warning: many people have had bad experiences with early versions of team building exercises. You may find some are skeptical and wary of being manipulated. For example, in the 1990s, corporate adventure-training programs were popular. These were often very physical and involved some pretty wild activities like paintball wars and ziplining. They flopped. Then, other team exercises went completely the opposite way. Many of those were built around a very popular personality assessment questionnaire that assigned everybody to one of sixteen personality types. They mostly flopped too.

Current team exercises are much more down-to-earth. Here are some general thoughts:

For your first activity, make it simple. You want your group to enjoy it and to see that it works. If several smaller exercises prove effective, you might consider doing a bit bigger (say, half-day) event. Hints:

- Advance planning is essential.
- Have a clearly defined objective and state what it is
- A good starting point would be revisiting your mission statement. Stress that the focus is on looking forward.
- Convey the attitude that team building is fun.

Avoid these situations at first:

- Role-play activities where most just watch
- Overly "touchy-feely" topics (stick to business)
- Handouts that are more than one page or too complex
- A very difficult problem — what fun is that?

Be sure to save some time at the end of the exercise for a wrap-up. This very important part is where all employees make a comment or two on their takeaways — what insight they're taking back to their job from the exercise.

A very important caveat: realize that you are probably not ready for a team building exercise if any of the following situations apply:

- There was a recent negative event, like the loss of a big client. The exercise might turn into a pity party and defeat the purpose.

- Trust issues are large, especially trust in you. This could have blowback.

- You sense that morale is low. You may be much better off starting with a simple Friday potluck lunch, and observing how that goes.

Here's a very simple example of a group development exercise. This can work well in a company where lots of change is occurring. All you need are pens and paper. Allow everyone three minutes to mentally choose an object in their office or workspace and then draw a sketch of it using the hand they don't normally use. Then, each person trades papers with another, who tries to figure out what it is. The discussion could be about how change is briefly uncomfortable but can be adapted to, or how a new task can be a fun challenge. It is also a fun way to demonstrate that even with a temporary handicap, you were still able to get your basic point across.

For next steps: Google "team building exercise" and see what looks appropriate for you. The local library will have several helpful books at call number 658.

Go ahead — and have some fun while you're at it!

36 THE P-O-L-C OF MANAGEMENT

QUESTION:

I'm pretty good with sales and marketing but I'm concerned that my weak management skills are holding my small business back. I think I need a crash course in "Management 101." Are there some basic management principles I can learn quickly? And how do I find out more?

ANSWER:

There's a simple concept in management basics that's appropriate for you and other small business operators.

Let's talk about this.

It's good that you realize you could benefit from having some additional management skills. When times are booming, it's easy to coast along doing whatever worked before. When that boom is more silent, it's a good time to beef up your managing skills. Remember that you're building for the long haul, not just for today.

The **P-O-L-C** model won't make you an instant MBA, but it will give you a managerial framework to try out. It's very generic. In this model, the four basic elements of management are **P**lanning, **O**rganizing, **L**eading, and **C**ontrolling. Let's look at each of these, with some examples.

Planning is a very important process where you, as the manager, define the company's objectives. You then lay out some particulars of how those goals will be achieved. This is commonly done by first outlining your vision for the company in a mission statement and then engaging in strategic planning, which defines the tactics for how the business will succeed. These goals must be **S**pecific, **M**easurable, **A**ttainable, **R**elevant, and **T**imed (or SMART). Google "smart business objectives" for loads of ideas on this part of the process.

It's important to realize that, for a small business, planning is best done as an early-stage activity. You need to be adaptable and light on your feet — that's a major competitive advantage of being a small business — and it's good to have several alternative strategies ready to roll. This is because if something flops, it's much easier to move to a predefined Plan B than to rewind back toward the beginning and start over again. Some additional examples of planning activities:

- Lay out your objectives in a SMART one-page document.
- Create a basic marketing plan.
- Make a spreadsheet of likely financial projections.

The gold standard of planning is to have a written business plan with details of what you will do and how you will make the business succeed.

Organizing is about setting up your internal operating structure. How do you allocate resources and set up systems, departments, and other functional parts of the business? Some typical organizing actions:

- Structure the flow of your goods or services — how they are made, marketed, sold, and delivered.
- Establish your human resources policies and procedures. This may include an organizational chart and employee handbook where appropriate.
- Set up, maintain, and update the accounting, cash-handling, and financial systems.

Leading is where you assemble your team and then help them succeed. Your business has an internal culture, even if you have just a few employees. This is where the rubber meets the road. You have a plan in place and an organizational structure, so now it's time to make it happen. Examples of typical leading actions:

- Be sure that you lead by example and are a team player too.

- Implement incentive and motivational programs.

- Address communication issues. This might mean a weekly staff meeting or an internal newsletter.

- Conduct performance appraisals. Managers hate doing these. Try to find an inventive way to deal with this, and the more frequently the better (see Section 33 on page 118). How about asking employees to do their own evaluation and then compare with yours?

Controlling is a critical function because if you can't measure it, you can't manage it. Some typical controlling functions:

- Monitor financial statements for trends or surprises. If you don't have accurate and prompt monthly financial statements, you're flying in the dark.

- Set up metrics. These are important financial or nonfinancial measures — for example, sales volume or new clients per month.

- Budget for future needs.

If this **P-O-L-C** model is of interest to you, here are several logical next steps:

- Check with your local community college for classes and workshops on small business.

- Numerous online sources can help you find what you need. Start at *sba.gov*, and click on the "Business Guide" tab.

- Google "free management training" and see what's of interest to you.

- For a SCORE counseling appointment, go to *score.org* and click on "Find a Mentor" to contact your local chapter. It's free and confidential.

- Your local library has loads of books on various management topics; look around call number 658.

And last, good for you, and carry on.

37 ARE WEEKLY STAFF MEETINGS STILL A GOOD IDEA?

QUESTION:
Our weekly staff meetings seem to be less productive than they used to be. Are there some ways to get back on track?

ANSWER:
Sounds like it's time for you to reevaluate what you're doing. There may be new and better ways for you to manage the internal communications aspect of your business.

Let's call a meeting to order and talk about this.

First off, given that you have likely attended numerous staff meetings over time, does it seem strange that you would now have trouble keeping yours interesting and productive? Well, you have lots of company. One reason is that we are all in communication overload. Things move fast and we all need to examine the old ways with an eye for opportunities to update them.

The staff meeting concept needs a good critical look. This may involve switching off the autopilot and trying something new. A small work group or team (say, five to eight people) is optimal for a fast-moving meeting with good results. Smaller or larger groups might need other approaches. A recent trend is to move away from the regularly scheduled, every-week time slot.

Remember, one option is not to have a meeting. This is part of "zero-based planning," where there is no meeting unless needed. Can you cover important points in an email? Do just a few people need to know about something? How about a memo, phone call, or text message? Use technology. If distance is an issue, consider videoconferencing by using Skype or Zoom. You'll cut down on wasted meeting time and restore your group's belief that the meetings they attend are necessary. Some managers report success having a weekly one-on-one meeting with each staffer and then, if needed, a monthly full-staff meeting.

The most common reason for meeting underperformance is a lack of clear objectives. Let's look at your goals for the meeting. Typically these include:

- Informing (downward communication)
- Gathering input (upward communication)
- Boosting morale and team spirit
- Announcing a budget, new policy, ad campaign, or other future item
- Making a choice or decision
- Providing specific training or skills

With your objectives clear, here are seven ideas for making your meetings more productive:

Go in with the right attitude. If you're tired of the meetings yourself, it's likely this will be apparent to your staff. Try to jazz it up a bit. Unless your business is life-and-death serious, why not have a little fun? Bring some food. Award a prize. Tell a joke.

Prepare adequately. As author Steven Covey notes, "Begin with the end in mind." Are your objectives clear to others? Are there any reading materials or data that should be distributed in advance? Is there a guest — for example, a sales rep — who would add interest for your staff?

Include only those who need to be there. At first, this may be uncomfortable, because some will feel left out. One way to handle this is to, yes, have a meeting. Tell the staff that productivity is very important now. It's best if everyone "(wo)man their post," whether that's working at their desk, dealing with clients, or making outside sales calls. Assure them they're not getting "de-looped" and that you will actually have more direct contact with them.

Pre-distribute a written agenda by email. Summarize the objectives of the meeting in an introductory paragraph. Consider structuring the meeting in segments. These are commonly 10-minute intervals. For example, two topics may take one segment each, and a third might take two segments. Put your most difficult agenda items in the middle of the meeting, when energy levels tend to be highest.

Consider rotating who leads the meeting. Include newer employees when ready. This is a chance for you to observe your staff in action, and also provides a developmental opportunity for employees.

Start on time and end on time. Don't allow distractions or side discussions. Be sure to schedule the meeting when it makes the most sense for your staff. A common time slot is Tuesday at 10:00 a.m. In the example above, everyone would know and plan for a four-segment meeting, or 40 minutes. Do a brief summary and wrap-up at the end.

Do appropriate follow-up. A brief rundown of major points and action items is enough; no need for lengthy minutes and formality. Distribute by email promptly after the meeting.

Staff meetings are consistently rated as the biggest time-waster in the workplace. You can take yours to another level. For more ideas, Google "staff meeting hints" and see what fits.

38 IMPROVING YOUR CREDIT REPORT AND FICO SCORE

QUESTION:

In a few months, I'll need to borrow money to buy some new equipment for my business. However, I fear that my credit report has blemishes and my credit score may be on the weak side. Are there some things I can do to improve my credit situation?

ANSWER:

Yes, there certainly are actions you can take to improve your credit, and there are some things you should definitely avoid doing.

Let's talk about this.

You're smart to start as soon as possible. Credit improvement is a slow process, and your credit information is now more important than ever because it is used for more than just qualifying for a bank loan. Other activities — like getting insurance coverage, determining the interest rate on a car loan, renting a house, or even getting a job — all may involve scrutiny of your credit history.

First off, recent laws make it much easier for you to access your personal credit information, but be careful about this. Many of those free credit report ads and websites have strings attached. Typically, the supposedly free credit report comes only with a paid subscription to a credit monitoring or similar service of questionable value.

The genuine, government-approved site is *annualcreditreport.com*, a joint effort of the three major credit reporting agencies, Equifax, Experian, and TransUnion. These agencies compete with each other for subscribers (banks and other credit grantors). The Fair and Accurate Credit Transactions (FACT) Act enables you to get your **credit report**, free, once a year from each of the three. Suggestion: a smart strategy is to rotate through the three agencies, ordering a report from one of them every four months.

As to your **credit score**, there are actually several of them, and they're not all created equal. The gold standard is the FICO score, which is issued by Fair Isaac Corporation based on their secret scoring system. Currently only Equifax offers the "real" FICO credit score, so start there. The additional fee is about $10. Several credit cards offer free credit reports and your FICO score monthly. You can also purchase your FICO score directly at *myfico.com*.

Start by getting your credit report and your FICO score, which will be between 300 and 850. A score over 780 is excellent. Over 720 is considered creditworthy. If your score is substantially below that, it's time to get to work. Go through the report with a fine-toothed comb, highlighting anything that looks unusual. Allocate some time for this because the report will contain information gathered over seven or more years.

A typical credit report has sections for the following:

- Your personal ID and information
- Summary of your credit accounts and payment history
- Public records

Make note of anything that may be incorrect. Consider this: the credit reporting agencies process around 5 billion pieces of data per month. If they do so with an error rate of 0.1 percent (pretty good!), then they are entering 5 million errors every month. It's likely you will find some errors in your report. If you want to contest an item in your credit report, submit a brief statement to the reporting agency by certified mail.

Some thoughts if you have a low credit score (below 600): beware of most of the credit repair or "credit doctor" offers. The Better Business Bureau (*bbb.org*) reports that there are thousands of complaints about these offers; many of them are outright scams. They commonly ask for up-front fees (which is illegal under the FACT Act) and may deliver no real value. Remember that no one else can do anything to fix your credit that you can't do. No one can remove valid negative data, only erroneous information. For the real deal, Google "consumer credit counseling services" and see what fits your needs.

The exact formula for the FICO score is a secret. Here's the best guess of what goes into that three-digit number that bears so strongly on our financial lives:

- Your on-time payment history: probably 35 percent
- Credit balances owed now as compared to available limits: 30 percent
- Overall credit history (borrowing patterns): 15 percent
- Types of credit owed (revolving, mortgages, etc.): 10 percent
- Number and type of recent credit requests: 10 percent

Based on that information, here's a list of ways to improve your credit:

- Pay all bills on time, especially installment debt. Never go over thirty days late.
- Always pay at least the minimum due monthly on credit cards.
- Keep your credit card debt under 35 percent of your available credit limit.
- Be stable and mixed in your borrowing habits — no surprises.
- Charge at least a small amount on several credit cards each month, and pay it off.
- Avoid applying for credit you don't really want, even if it offers an incentive.
- Don't close out paid-off credit cards, especially if they are long-established.

For more information and credit-improving hints, check out the Federal Trade Commission at *ftc.gov*, and click on the "Advice and Guidance" tab.

39 THE IMPORTANCE OF NEGOTIATING SKILLS

QUESTION:
I'm concerned that my negotiating skills are a bit weak. It seems like I come out on the short end of deals way more often than I should. What can I do about this?

ANSWER:
You might need to beef up your bargaining skills. You won't become a master wheeler-dealer overnight, but some basics are easy to learn.

Let's talk about this.

This talent can be very important to your success. Your negotiating skills can mean the difference between your business just getting by and really thriving. We'll look at some of the background issues, a few basic negotiating styles, and some negotiating fundamentals. Then you'll learn about some common negotiating tactics. We'll also look at some devious and unethical tactics, and discuss how to realize if they're being used on you.

Anybody who's been in business will probably tell you that it is a constant process of negotiation. This may be with vendors, suppliers, regulatory offices, taxing agencies, employees, a landlord, or a neighboring business. It's ongoing.

There's professional training available, if you're so inclined. The top dog in negotiation training for over fifty years is Karrass Effective Negotiating seminars. They claim that over 1,000,000 business professionals worldwide have attended their training. Their basic instruction is a two-day class that costs around $1,200. Their website (*karrass.com*) has informative tips, including an excellent and comprehensive negotiation glossary. Their great tagline: "You don't get what you deserve, you get what you negotiate."

To start off, try thinking of negotiating as a general life skill. Everybody negotiates every day. Of course, at different stages of life, the issues and stakes are different. Consider these examples: a child asking permission for a sleepover, a teen wanting to get her driver's license, a couple deciding when and where to get married, or the family discussing what to watch on movie night. Note that these issues aren't primarily about money or business — just life events.

Also, negotiation is not only about resolving disagreement and conflict. In a successful situation, both parties end up getting something they value more highly than what they gave up. That's the classic win-win type of deal.

Two recent trends have tossed some new wrinkles into our lives. First, the globalization of business now makes it more likely that you will be interacting with people from different cultures. You must be sensitive to how other cultures interact with yours. It may surprise you, but there are many common American-style behaviors that have different and often very negative, meanings to people from other cultures. Examples:

- Crossing your legs or exposing the sole of your shoe
- Arriving late (this is a serious insult in some cultures)
- Pointing
- Improper informality, like immediate use of first names
- Prolonged eye contact
- Excessive concern about your personal space
- Neglecting to bring a small gift

If this interests you, go to *negotiationtraining.com.au/articles* and scroll down to "Cultural Negotiation Boundaries."

Second, much of internet communication deprives you of important information (visual and auditory) about whom you're dealing with.

It's generally thought that there are five basic negotiating styles. Most people have more than one of them, depending on the circumstances and on how skilled and experienced they are. Think about what mix of these styles you have:

- **Avoiding.** Avoiders dislike conflicts and avoid them whenever possible. Their M.O. is to sidestep or postpone the issue, hoping for some other resolution. Reaching agreement with an avoider can be very difficult.

- **Compromising.** The priority of compromisers is to maintain a productive relationship. They will propose a compromise early, giving the other person what they want in order to reach an agreement and preserve the relationship.

- **Accommodating.** Accommodators hope to resolve conflict by solving the other person's problems. If the other person is also an accommodator, then he or she returns the favor and helps solve the first person's problems. If not, the other person takes and gives nothing in return.

- **Competing.** Competitors like to prevail and be in control of the situation. They believe that if they win, then you lose — and they like that. "My way or the highway."

- **Collaborating or problem solving.** These are the imaginative thinkers who create fair win-win solutions and greater outcomes that make the pie bigger.

For some help with structuring an upcoming negotiation, go to the excellent Mind Tools website (*mindtools.com*) and click on "Explore", then "Business Skills", and then "Strategy Tools."

Here are four negotiation fundamentals:

1. The single best thing you can do to have a successful negotiation is define your goals very clearly before you go in. This keeps you focused on what matters and less susceptible to being dragged onto things that don't.

2. Another important negotiation issue you need to know about is information asymmetry. This is where the other party brings to the table much more and better knowledge of the situation than you do. This can be a real problem so be careful. The absolute

worst case is where you "don't know what you don't know." The minute you sense this, bow out and do some research.

3. The old accepted wisdom was always to force the other party to give the first number. The idea here was that it established your dominance in the negotiation. Problem is, if everybody did this, nothing would ever happen. The new thinking is to use "anchoring." This is where you get your number out for discussion, and then the negotiation works from there. You can choose how to work the deal from your own starting point.

4. Human nature is to assume that the other side is fair and well-intentioned. If you're dealing with someone you don't know, here's a suggestion: clarify this before you start. State up front that you need their agreement that you're both bargaining in good faith. If they later raise a point that is a bit farfetched, you can say, "Whoa, you said you are here in good faith … What gives?"

Here are five examples of common and legitimate negotiation tactics:

The flinch. This tactic is just what it sounds like. The moment you mention a price or other important term, the other party visibly flinches and makes an "ooh" sound as if they've been poked with a pin.

Standard forms. This is often used in purchase contracts and other documents. The other side tells you, "Our legal department prepared this for you to sign; you can't change anything."

The salami-slice tactic. This is where you're asked for a small concession, and then another and another. It's effective where grabbing the whole salami would be too obvious.

Nonverbal cues. These subtleties are a topic all their own. Google "business body language" for loads of info.

Silence. A skilled negotiator uses brief pauses and silence to best advantage. The general guideline to shoot for is to do one-third talking, two-thirds listening. If the other party clams up, don't feel like you have to fill in.

Here are five devious tactics to be alert for:

Over questioning. Of course there will be questions but keep a balance to make sure you're not being played or manipulated. For example, if you're questioned repeatedly about the features of your product, you might respond, "Tell me more about what features you're looking for."

Good cop/bad cop. It's so obvious. If you sense this, get out immediately. Say, "Sorry, I can only deal with one of you, or else we're done here."

Home court advantage. If the other party insists on controlling the negotiating environment, it's a clear warning signal. Stories abound of hardball negotiators. You might end up in a small uncomfortable chair with the light in your face while your counterpart has a tall chair behind a big desk.

Angry bluster. You may be subjected to a fake outburst in an attempt to throw you off guard.

Bogus limited authority. You strike a deal but the other party now says they have to get final approval from someone else. If you think this might be a possibility, ask up front, "Can I assume we both have the authority to make a deal right now?"

A last, important thought: if it becomes clear that a good outcome is very unlikely, don't be afraid to end the discussion. It's better to have no deal than a bad one.

40 EMPLOYEE RETENTION

QUESTION:
Recently, I talked with a business owner who had high employee turnover. In contrast, my employees are a pretty solid group, but I'm looking for some ways to motivate them to stay on board. I can't pay big bucks for salaries so are there some other ways to give them incentives to stick with me?

ANSWER:
Yes, there are dozens of ways to motivate employees and build loyalty without breaking the bank.

Let's talk about this.

Just so you know, human resources professionals generally consider that a comprehensive reward system has four main components. The two hard areas are wages and benefits. The two soft areas are recognition and appreciation.

We're not going to discuss formal programs like employee stock options or profit-sharing plans here. Instead, we'll focus on some less formal incentives and on using rewards and other fun techniques that have proven to be effective, fairly low in cost, and appropriate to most small businesses.

Warning: it's very tempting to jump into this the wrong way — backwards. This could happen when you hear about an innovative employee reward plan, for example, and then try to force-fit it into your business. The right way is to take a moment to define your objectives. What behaviors would you like to see more, or less, of? What kinds of opportunities would you like to have your employees bring to you?

Here are the five currently most popular and effective employee incentive programs, all at little cost. See what ideas you might be able to adapt for your business.

Health and wellness programs. These have been common at the corporate and governmental levels for years. Lately, smaller companies are adopting them with innovative ideas tuned to small business. Check out the federal Centers for Disease Control and Prevention (*cdc.gov*) for information about their Workplace Health Initiatives. Healthy employees have higher productivity and lower absenteeism.

Typical examples:

- Company-sponsored gym memberships, with discounts for family members
- Quit-smoking or weight-loss assistance; confidential mental health counseling
- A small library of health-related materials, including workout videos and healthy recipe books
- Secure bike storage, introduced with a "Bike-to-Work Week" event

Flextime and telework scheduling. Consider these very popular arrangements, if appropriate to your business model. Flextime allows certain employees to self-select their working hours, as long as they're at work during the core hours, typically 9 a.m. to 2 p.m. Telework (also called telecommuting) allows an employee to work from a home office for some agreed-on part of the time. For more on these topics, Google the two terms.

Suggestion box awards. This idea has been around for decades, and it's been underused by American small businesses. It may surprise you that in Japan, suggestion box ideas are commonly solicited and highly rewarded. A typical Japanese employee might make fifty suggestions a year. To make this effective, you'll have to manage it carefully. Here are some tips for doing this:

- Make up a simple preprinted form. Have sections for the date, a brief statement of the problem or opportunity, suggestions to make it better, and other comments. Submissions can be anonymous or signed.

- Empty the box weekly. Look the submissions over and then award a prize by a random drawing from all of the valid and signed suggestions. A gift card to a local restaurant is an example of a typical prize.

- Consider special recognition for an idea that identifies a significant waste or inefficiency, or some other fixable problem.

Training and educational opportunities. Tuition reimbursement plans have become very common. Your employee asks to take a class on a business topic or other relevant subject. If you agree, the typical plan reimburses employees for tuition and necessary books at local educational outlets.

The internet has really opened up this area. Example: an amazing online learning resource, Khan Academy (*khanacademy.org*), has thousands of training videos on a variety of topics. Browse their offerings on business and think about how you might use these videos for your employee development.

Workplace fun. Some ideas:

- Order in a pizza lunch now and then.

- Have a random drawing for who gets a paid day off next month.

- Hold an awards meeting for a special employee accomplishment.

- Open a staff meeting with a workplace-appropriate joke.

Google "workplace fun ideas" for thousands more possibilities.

For more information, go to *ehow.com* and enter "employee incentive program." Closing thought: happy employees are a very powerful recruiting tool.

STAGE FIVE:
RENEWAL OR DECLINE

Revisit your Key Performance Initiatives for a look at how you're doing on your objectives. Don't be afraid of making changes; they're going to happen anyway.

Introductory Thoughts

- Phase out any goods or services that are underperforming.
- Use social media to the fullest.
- Realize that all products and services have a life cycle. Gently add some new goods and services that show promise. Innovate!
- Transition to your exit strategy if appropriate.
- If you have the slightest thought that you're sinking, get help PRONTO.

41 CREATIVITY AND INNOVATION IN BUSINESS

QUESTION:
I own a business. It's doing OK. Although I realize that innovation is an important part of business success, I'm not very creative. Are there some ways for me to learn this skill, or am I doomed to be a dud forever?

ANSWER:
You can and should learn ways to add innovation to your business skill set. A great many businesses find that there is a plateau after a few years when things become a bit routine and stagnant. Being quick to adapt is very important. It used to be the big that eat the small; now it's the fast (the innovators) that eat the slow.

Let's talk about this.

The main finding of a study by IBM involving 1,541 CEOs from sixty countries was that CEOs believe that "more than rigor, management discipline, integrity, or even vision, successfully navigating an increasingly complex world will require creativity."

Sounds like you need a jump-start. First off, let's step back and look at what creativity is. Some call it a left-brain/right-brain deal. And this isn't just psychobabble. It's backed by an established body of neurological and psychological research. This theory says that the dominantly left-brained people include the concrete thinkers like accountants and engineers. On the other side are the right-brainers — the artists, musicians, and inventors. Sounds like you're definitely not in this latter group.

It's time to look in the mirror and see if you're comfortable becoming an innovator, a synthesizer, an originator. Here's one test — do you frequently think of new ideas for your business? Can you visualize a new and different future not just in three years but also in three months, or three weeks? Innovations don't have to be brand new products or services — it's an incremental process. This may be a slightly new way of doing business — for example, revamping your website. Or a new market you might pursue, like older or younger customers. Or even a new approach to your internal operations, like adopting Lean business practices.

One huge advantage of small businesses is that they're nimble. When you're fast on your feet, you can outcompete larger firms, which are not as adaptable. For example, if you see a changing local market opportunity, you can pivot much faster than a large company. You don't have several layers of management to run the idea up the flagpole. Plus, a fast pivot means that you can get out just as quickly if the idea doesn't work, with minimal losses.

Let's review the concepts of creativity and innovation and note how they are related — but not the same.

- **Creativity** is a process where you or others come up with original ideas that could improve your business. These ideas may be ones you think about for a while, or they may drop out of the sky. We'll look at some techniques for doing this in a moment. Think of creativity as being the "front end" for innovation. It's necessary, but it's not sufficient.

- **Innovation** implements that creativity by coupling it with execution. Sounds heavy, but it basically means that you have to actually put selected ideas into reality.

There's a new business concept about this: it's called being a "reinventor." This suggests that your business must continuously evolve new products, services, and markets. This might be scary for a low-innovation company or owner. But there's always a backstop. Keep in mind that just like many other business skills, creativity can be rented. Ad agencies, marketing firms, freelance consultants, and others will be happy to give you their ideas, of course for a fee.

If you and your employees are locked into tunnel vision, you may miss opportunities to out innovate the competition. Here are some ways to avoid that fate:

- Switch from a "Yes, but …" to a "Yes, and …" approach.

- Consider using techniques like brainstorming and lateral thinking exercises if your staff needs a little help.

- Be clear that you're open to new ideas. This could have a side benefit of attracting and retaining highly creative employees who are more comfortable in a less-restrained work environment.

- Walk the talk. If you're serious about innovation, accept that there is risk of failure. Not every new idea is a winner.

- Remember that to think outside the box, you have to step outside the box.

There are loads of ways to improve your creativity skills. Google keywords like these: "brainstorming"; "mind mapping"; "using suggestion box"; "lateral thinking puzzles"; "business improv class"; "business creativity exercises." Also check out an excellent book, *Zero to One: Notes on Startups, or How to Build the Future*, by Peter Thiel.

42 DON'T MISS OUT ON KHAN ACADEMY

QUESTION:
I've heard several mentions of something called Khan Academy. I looked into it, and I'm totally blown away by its potential for educating myself and my employees. Why don't more people know about it? And what's the latest scoop?

ANSWER:
You got it right. I'm a huge proponent of Khan Academy —it's an astounding learning and employee-development resource. Every business owner and manager should become familiar with it, and then think of ways to use it to best advantage in their own business.

Let's talk about this.

First off, let's be clear about what we're discussing. Khan Academy (KA) is a nonprofit educational organization. Their free website has thousands of brief instructional videos on a variety of subjects. Note: in this case, "free" actually means … free. No registration, no login, no account setup (unless you want to track your progress). Their mission statement: "To provide a free, world-class education for anyone, anywhere." This could be a real game changer for the American education system.

All you need to do is go to the website, *khanacademy.org*, and look over the class offerings. You will be surprised by the variety. Maybe you want to learn more about some aspect of algebra, or biology, or art history, or business and economics topics. They're all there. A typical video runs about ten minutes. They range in level from fairly basic (in beginning math) to quite complex (in the sciences).

Here's the backstory, a great illustration of how entrepreneurship works. Salman Khan is an amazing guy. He started out in 2006 with an idea about helping people learn. Now the 45-year-old American has been called "the most watched teacher in the world." From his small-scale beginnings — he recorded his first videos in a closet — Khan attracted the attention, and then money, of some heavyweights. Bill Gates was so impressed he chipped in $1.5 million. Google came in with $2 million. Realize that these are outright donations, not equity investments.

Khan has three degrees from MIT and an MBA from Harvard Business School. He developed and posted his very first videos on YouTube to help his cousin (1,200 miles away) with her homework. To give you some idea of scale, recently the KA channel on YouTube had more than 7 million subscribers, and the videos have been viewed more than 1.9 billion times.

As you'll see, Khan himself doesn't appear on camera in the videos. Instead, the viewer watches and listens as Khan draws diagrams, solves equations, sketches out ideas (Khan-cepts?), and roughs out key principles directly on the screen. Khan's narration is very informal, as if he is making it up on the fly, which is what he often does. He doesn't edit his recordings; if he doesn't like the result, he does it over.

At first, there was some pushback from the established educational community. This has subsided. One reason is KA's development of a "dashboard" display, which allows a classroom teacher to monitor, in real time, each student's progress at a glance. This includes not just their advancement through lessons and applying the knowledge while at school, but also each student's progress while online at home. Three groups are eagerly becoming major users of KA: charter schools, home-schooling parents, and summer enrichment camps.

KA may bring about an advancement in traditional learning. It's a new idea called the "flipped classroom." For decades, schools have used the lecture style of instruction, and then the students do homework for the next day on their own. The KA model flips this around. Students learn at their own pace at home, and then come in to the classroom for individualized help. Many teachers are delighted at the prospect of not having to teach to the middle. If students have trouble absorbing the material, they can review it online as needed. This avoids holding up the rest of the class for additional explanation or, just as bad, passing over a student's needs so others can move along.

Here's a way you might try this out in your business. Look through KA offerings and note some that might help your staff. Tell those who qualify that you'll pay them $1 a minute for one class a week. So for a typical 10-minute class, you'll add $10 to their weekly gross pay. Another thought: have each staffer write up a twenty-word summary of the video, and present it at your staff meeting.

Salman Khan has given us two things: a terrific learning opportunity, and a great example of turning an idea into a successful business.

43 SHOULD I GO TO A TRADE SHOW?

> **QUESTION:**
> *Several other businesspeople have mentioned going to a trade show, saying that it was very helpful and interesting. Is this something I should look into?*
>
> **ANSWER:**
> *Think about your skill sets for a moment. As a businessperson, you have specific knowledge in one or more fields. Perhaps you are in a retail trade, sell a particular service, or have a professional license of some sort. Lots of other similar people do too, and they'd like to meet with you. And even better, the hundreds of folks who sell to you would like to put on a big show and have you all attend ... usually for free!*
>
> *Let's talk about this.*

First, we need to be clear here. If you've been to the local home show, or a regional boat show, or an RV Show ... those are NOT trade shows. Those are consumer shows (B2C — business-to-consumer). They're open to the public.

Trade shows, on the other hand, are open only to businesspeople in relevant fields. A trade show is B2B (business-to-business). Admission is only with an ID badge from preregistration. Children are generally not allowed. It's all about business.

Some trade shows are very large. Each January, the Consumer Electronics Show in Las Vegas sees over 150,000 people over four days. The top standard venue in trade shows is McCormick Place in Chicago. This facility has 2.6 million square feet of expo space across all levels. The National Restaurant Association Show in Chicago has had 2,100 exhibitors. Over 74,000 people attended from all fifty states and 110 countries. Of course, a smaller show closer to home may make more sense for you.

There are three basic parts to a trade show:

- After clearing registration, you'll go in to the **show floor**. This huge room has hundreds of booths for exhibitors to show off their products and services. They want to attract your attention to what they have to show. That may be a new product or service, or some other way to make your business better.

- Numerous **side rooms** typically have breakout meetings where companies present training sessions, new product unveilings, or similar insider information. This is a great opportunity to have one-on-one conversations with sales reps and others who may be helpful to you. It's good for both of you to have a face to put with a name in future discussions.

- Companies sponsor **hospitality suites**, often in a connected hotel, where you're invited, schmoozed, and beveraged — and get to meet company officials.

It's also common to have luncheon and dinner events with a keynote speaker. This is typically someone of fame or notoriety in the field, perhaps a major business or brand owner. Steve Jobs was famous for doing Apple's new product intros at trade shows.

Of course, the whole point of the show is to generate business for the exhibitors. Some trade shows (for example, those for gift, apparel, and furniture retailers) are buying shows. At these shows, a retailer might see products of interest and issue purchase orders (POs) for several months worth of goods, or more. This is called "bringing the PO book." Exhibitors may offer special show discounts or delayed billing (dating). It's a good use of time for all.

A few hints for your show attendance:

- Preregister early, online. Your entry badge and information will arrive online or in the mail. Registering on-site when you get there is crowded and wastes time.

- Wear business casual clothing and comfortable shoes. Plan on walking and talking a lot and having some fun.

- Bring a ton of business cards to hand out. This is a great and inexpensive way to make a lasting impression. It's also a good conversation starter.

- When you're at the booths and exhibits, have exhibitors scan the barcode on your ID badge for your contact info. Then a company rep can contact you for further discussion.

- You'll likely meet some competitors while you're there. What a great opportunity to show how classy you are.

- Don't be shy about introducing yourself to the big suppliers and players in your business. They need you as much as you need them.

- Make sure you bring a suitcase that has ample extra room in it. This is to bring home the literature, samples, promotional products, etc. you will get from the vendors.

To find out more about trade shows, take a look online. Google "trade show [your business field])" and see what comes up.

44 PRODUCT LIFE CYCLE

QUESTION:

My small business relies on just a few goods and services that we offer. How can I predict how long each will remain viable and competitive? How will I foresee their decline? What should I know about this?

ANSWER:

You are right to be concerned. Every business product and service has a finite life cycle and they all go through fairly predictable stages. You need to look a long way ahead and start to adapt, as needed, right now.

Let's talk about this.

First, we need to be clear that "product life cycle" refers not just to a physical item, but also to a work product, like a service that your business offers. Even if you only resell goods made by others, it's still important that you understand the life cycle concept.

Here are some examples. A very long-life-cycle product: the household electric refrigerator. They've been around in some form for about 100 years, because they have evolved to meet their users' needs. A very long-lived service product: architectural design. Again, this service evolved from the old pencil-and-paper era, through tremendous internal change, into current CAD technology. Note that the word "evolved" occurs in both descriptions of long-lived products.

Example of a short-lived product: the Pet Rock. A short-cycle service example: social media site *theGlobe.com* (you might have forgotten that one). Both of these had their big moments and then promptly disappeared.

So why do some products and services have long and profitable life cycles while others flame out and die? In short, a product or service starts out as an idea, is developed into reality, grows, matures, and then declines. Here are some details of these stages and how they play out:

Concepting and origination. At the front end of any successful new product or service is a person who notices a need and devises a way to fill it. Once the concept is defined, it's time for the research and development work.

Initial development. Part of product development must include an analysis of all of the costs to bring the product to market. This includes sourcing, packaging, and loads of other issues.

If your business resells goods made by others, your development is constantly monitoring your offerings for something better. If you run a service business, you need to continuously develop new and desired services.

Occasionally a large firm will overdo their brand extension, often with comical results. Actual launched products: Smith & Wesson mountain bikes, Colgate frozen entrees, Bic underwear, Harley Davidson perfume.

Launch and growth. Putting the product out to market means that some sales revenue is coming in! Slowly at first, then faster as the product or service gains popularity. The growth stage is fun and exciting, but be careful. Think about consumer electronics over the last couple decades: hundreds of devices that were introduced have exploded in sales and popularity. Thousands of others have vanished.

Maturity. Here's where your highest profit lies. As sales level off, the game becomes to sustain the product and postpone its decline. Meanwhile, it's time to get some new offerings into the pipeline for future development. Don't wait until the stage of decline.

The role of innovation looms large here. A product or service can enjoy an extended maturity if you can add new features, usability, or convenience. This is also a good time to try new markets, including exporting, because your costs are known and minimized. Increased competition may drive prices down, putting the squeeze on profitability.

A main reason the refrigerator has enjoyed an extremely long maturity stage is because there have been continuous improvements in features, price, quality, and efficiency. Consider this: in 1922, a home refrigerator cost about $725, while a new 1922 Ford Model T cost $450. Today you can buy a mid-level fridge for $725, but a very basic new car is at least $15,000.

Decline. At some point, most every product and service will eventually weaken in market appeal, and sales will fall. At this stage, you will have to decide if you want to try some rescue CPR, or let it go and move on. If you don't have a developing stream of new offerings, you're in trouble.

Think about this: the advice that you must "always listen to your customers" may be too limited. New suggestion: it's also important to listen to your noncustomers. These are the people who are **not** buying your products and services. Wouldn't it be important to find out why? Did they buy them before, but not now? Did they consider them, but not buy? Did they buy a competing product, and if so, why?

The takeaway lesson is that your product and service offerings have to be continuously evolving and adapting to your customers' changing needs. For more thoughts, Google "product life cycle" and see what interests you.

45 WATCH FOR SIGNS OF BURNOUT

QUESTION:

My business is humming right along. I've heard horror stories about some very bad consequences of entrepreneur burnout. That sounds really harsh. How would I know if this is happening to me and what can I do if I think it's coming my way?

ANSWER:

There are lots of stressful aspects of starting and running a small business. However, while stress is expected and can even be a pretty good motivator, end-stage burnout is entirely different and destructive. That's where you tank your business, dump your employees, hose your creditors, and trash your credit. It's ugly.

Let's talk about this.

First off, we need to differentiate between stress and burnout. Stress comes from things like wearing many hats, dealing with cash flow problems, finding new clients and customers, supervising and directing employees, working long hours, and all the unknowns about developing and offering your goods and services. These are pretty normal small business concerns.

Consider this: when you start your own business, you give up the ability to quit. That may sound silly, but everybody who works for someone else has a comforting safety valve: they can hike. You can't, without some pretty grave consequences. In other words, stress comes with running a small business. Certainly, things like stress, overload, time pressure, and other factors can be precursors to burnout — but they don't necessarily cause it.

Burnout, on the other hand, is much more serious. To make this distinction crystal clear, stress is "Wow, I'm completely overloaded!" End-stage burnout is "I don't care anymore."

Here are four burnout danger signals to look for. Note that these occur over time; you may not even realize what's happening. Beware of these signs:

Abandonment of work-life balance. If you're spending numerous long days at your business while you have a spouse and kids at home, you should reevaluate this. Same if you are ignoring other people, like parents and friends — or even yourself.

Loss of motivation. If you've come to feel like it isn't worth it, that's a bad sign. Sit down with a sheet of paper and make a list of some things you enjoy about your life and business. If several minutes pass and you haven't written much down, that's a warning signal.

Depression, or overuse of alcohol or drugs in an effort to combat it.

Health issues. These might include unusual weight gain or loss, sleeping problems, or lowered immunity.

If you think you're headed toward burnout, get help immediately. Confide in a trusted friend or get professional help for your business and yourself.

Here are some ways to fend off burnout:

Break your old daily pattern. If you typically get up, quickly do your morning activities, and then rush out the door, here's an easy suggestion: get up fifteen minutes earlier, sit in a comfy chair and read a book. View this as your personal time — no calls, no interruptions.

Ramp up your family and social ties. Being socially engaged is a great way to have a healthy perspective about your life and your business.

Work from a daily to-do list. This seems obvious, but if you get dragged into troubleshooting and response mode, your original goals and objectives can get pushed into second place. Book in some time for things you may not have foreseen, but don't allow the "tyranny of the urgent" to overrule what's actually important.

Learn to view a customer complaint or problem as an opportunity. Here's how one very successful restaurant operator sees it: look at a complaint as a gift package. When a customer hands it to you, thank the person sincerely. He says the reason it's a gift is that it gives you four things:

- The opportunity to fix it — this retains the customer and generates good will

- A teachable moment — the server who brought you the complaint sees you addressing it comfortably

- Awareness and feedback about a potential problem in your business

- A bonus — you can learn how to take a complaint and respond professionally (realizing it isn't a personal attack on you)

Choose your battles carefully. A smart manager knows that it's better to lose a battle in order to win the war. Also note that choosing to not fight a battle you think you'll lose is a sign of wisdom, not weakness.

If you're concerned that you may be headed down the burnout path, there are several good self-assessment tools available. One good general checklist is at *mindtools.com*; enter "burnout self-test" in the search box. Also, you can Google "entrepreneur burnout" for more information.

46 WHAT DO I NEED TO KNOW ABOUT IRS AUDITS?

QUESTION:
I file my federal income tax return every year with the IRS but I'm terrified of being audited. What's the inside scoop on IRS audits and how can I reduce my apprehension about it?

ANSWER:
You have "audit anxiety." It's an important part of our voluntary compliance system. The IRS uses audit anxiety to help keep taxpayers honest. But of course, there's more to the story.

Let's talk about this.

First off, we need to dial the stress level down a little. Here's the deal. If you've heard horror stories about the "audit from hell," you can relax a bit. Years ago, the IRS had an ugly program called the Taxpayer Compliance Measurement Program (TCMP). This program selected about 50,000 returns each year for comprehensive audit, and demanded that the taxpayer prove literally every detail of every line on their tax return. The TCMP audits were so intrusive and hated that Congress demanded a kinder and gentler approach. The National Research Program is the replacement.

There are two main reasons for all of this analysis. One is that the IRS wants to know where people fudge their numbers. Also, the feds want to be able to estimate what they call the "tax gap." This concept describes the difference between what taxpayers report and pay, and what the IRS thinks they actually owe. The most recent estimate of the tax gap is about $1 trillion annually. Over 80 percent of the gap derives from the underreporting of income and the overreporting of expenses.

We'll take a quick look at several different types of audits. Then, we'll review some examples of common audit triggers. These are the red flags that the IRS computers spot while processing your forms.

There are three common types of audits. Ongoing technology developments are changing this, but here are the basics. A **correspondence audit** typically involves a letter from the IRS asking for clarification or additional documentation in support of something in your return. An **office audit** asks that you come in to the IRS office and bring certain documents or other information. A **field audit** is more suitable for larger companies. The auditor arranges for a visit to the business, seeking additional or clarifying information.

The recent overall audit rate for all individual returns is about 1 percent. But of course, more scrutiny is given to higher-income filers. For example, returns showing income of $1 million or more were audited at around a 10 percent rate.

In general, the IRS can audit back for three years, though under certain circumstances they can go back further. The limit is six years if they assert that you've omitted substantial income. Get professional help with any audit issue you're unsure of.

As each tax return is processed by computer, it is assigned a score. This is sort of a sniff test that compares the information entered on the return with the database of other similar returns. You may hear this called a "DIF score." Those returns with high DIF scores are pulled for further examination. The exact factors and formulas the IRS uses for audit selection are top secret.

Here are eight common reasons for additional scrutiny:

- **Underreporting income.** The IRS matches essentially all W-2s and 1099s with the taxpayer's return. If you don't report documented income, the document matching program will flag the error.

- **Operating a cash business.** Firms that handle cash get extra analysis. Examples: beauty shops, restaurants and bars, taxicabs.

- **Claiming large charitable contributions.** The IRS has imposed restrictions on what used to be a free-for-all. The most recent crackdown was on donations of used cars at inflated values.

- **Using many round numbers.** If you file a Schedule C and a lot of the expense amounts are in round thousands, your DIF score will light up.

- **Reporting very low income in an expensive zip code.** This may be a valid situation, but there's a flag here. The IRS will ask you this question: "What is the source of the money on which you live?"

- **Claiming recurrent business losses.** This may flag your business as a hobby. This means no loss deductions unless you can refute it.

- **Overstating business expenses for meals and entertainment.** A partial deduction is allowed for legitimate business meal expenses. This means a reasonable meal with a current or prospective customer.

- **Using a "problem preparer."** The IRS has a list of tax return preparers who have been problematic. Recent laws require preparers to undergo certification.

Hope this eases your anxiety. For further info, contact your local IRS office; check *irs.gov* for downloadable forms and publications.

47 BASICS OF DELEGATING

QUESTION:
My small business is stable but not growing. I have only very basic skills at delegating duties to my employees. I want to become a better manager of people. Is there a new method or technique that I should know about?

ANSWER:
Yes, there is. The ability to delegate effectively is a vital management skill. It allows you to leverage yourself and accomplish much more than you could otherwise. It can make or break your business.

Let's talk about this.

Effective delegation is a cornerstone of good management and it helps develop your people. In delegating, as opposed to just assigning a duty, you are loaning some of your authority to an employee. Fun idea: think of delegation as internal outsourcing.

It's important that you know about the five levels of freedom to act. Picture each employee having a rank at this moment. Here's a quick review of the five levels, from highest to lowest:

- **Act on own.** These employees are your superstars. At this high level, you are basically giving them the authority to act in your place. These people are the most highly trusted members of your staff.

- **Act, then inform.** This level also has a high level of trust and autonomy. The employee has freedom to take action, but then needs to advise you of the action taken and its outcome.

- **Recommend, then act.** This is a more junior level of authority. This employee is dependable and responsible, but has a shorter leash in terms of their authority. Typically, many good employees are at this level.

- **Ask what to do.** Example: a recent or inexperienced hire. Best bet is to help them move up a notch to "Recommend, then act" as soon as they are able, or to wash them out.

- **Wait until told.** This might be a temporary hire or a semi-employee like a college intern.

Note that the two lowest levels have an important difference; they are commonly called "the freedom to do nothing." You don't want employees to be in these levels for very long.

The new view of delegation is not like the old way of just giving orders. It's much more like a collaboration, where you and the employee discuss the task, what resources are needed, and how it can be completed and measured. In management terms, this is often called "defining the deliverable." Over time you should come to view delegation as a win-win situation. Think of it as a form of empowerment where your staff gets increasing responsibility and gains new skills and your business gets increased efficiency and productivity.

There's a simple and effective way to structure delegation, often mentioned as the acronym SMARTER. In this framework, the key attributes of delegation are that it be Specific, Measurable, Agreed, Realistic, Timebound, Ethical, and Recorded. Here are some details on this technique; see how it might fit for you.

Specific. In delegation, it's very important that the manager and employee both understand exactly what is expected. For a sizable task, you should prepare written details about task outcomes. Brief example: "Increase export sales by 10 percent next year."

Measurable. It's counterproductive to propose vague and unmeasurable outcomes. If you can't define the outcome in clear terms, you haven't thought it through adequately. Your metric could be financial or something else — for example, "Add five new clients each month."

Agreed. The whole point of delegation is that everybody involved buys in. Be sure that all essential players are informed, involved, and committed. You can't delegate a job to someone without also giving the person the tools (financial, staffing, and otherwise) to accomplish it.

Realistic. As you decide whom to assign the task to, look at the "skill and will" of the candidates. Is this something that those you are entrusting with the task can do with their skills and experience, with the available resources, and within the expected time frame? Be honest with yourself and them about these matters.

Timebound. An open-ended plan that lacks a defined endpoint or deadline is not motivating. Time, like any other resource, has value and has to be factored in.

Ethical. You can't ask an employee to do something that is unethical or that you wouldn't do yourself.

Recorded. Keep a few brief notes about the task, how it progressed, the timeline, any interim milestones, and how it was completed. Also note any significant errors or trouble spots that came up along the way.

As you use the SMARTER delegation technique, keep this in mind: "Great leaders gain authority by giving it away." —Admiral James Stockdale.

48 DECEMBER BUSINESS CHALLENGES

QUESTION:

I'm concerned that December is a demanding month for managing a business. In particular, I'm looking at staff scheduling issues. I'm also considering having a small holiday party now that my business can afford it. What do you think?

ANSWER:

Yes, December is a challenge. It may seem like everyone wants time off for travel to relatives, religious observances, or various other purposes. Plus, the holiday party you mentioned demands that you go in with your eyes open and fully aware of some potential problems. And to pile on, there are several other December challenges.

Let's talk about this.

As to the **staffing** matter, it depends greatly on the nature of your business. For most retailers, it's gotta be "all hands on deck" to staff the store. Many personal service businesses are in full marketing mode in December to sell their services, and also gift cards to fuel future purchases. On the other hand, some professional service firms — for example, an architect's office — might well decide to end the work year on December 20.

Just who gets the highly desired days off could be determined by seniority, or you might have a lottery-style drawing or some other way to decide who can be absent. Of course, this depends on your workload, the structure of the business, and the needs of your customers and clients.

Holiday parties are still very popular. Among larger firms, around three-fourths have some kind of a holiday party or function. Some are converting to employees only functions and others are holding the event as an extended lunch. If this interests you, Google "Battalia Winston Survey."

One concern, and a fairly common occurrence at company parties, is overindulgence in alcoholic beverages. Human resources departments and others who follow these matters offer several reasons for this:

- The party's social atmosphere is charged up because it's the holiday season, the year end, and a chance to interact informally with coworkers.
- The beverage servers may not be trained bartenders and thus may not be good at recognizing people who have been overserved.
- Since drinks are free, there's a "bring it on" mentality.
- Some people may not imbibe at other times during the year and don't know their limits.

This problem is widespread. A large human resources firm, Adecco Staffing USA, surveyed a sample of American workers on this exact issue. The survey of 1,000 respondents yielded these results:

- "I know someone who has been reprimanded by their employer for their behavior at a holiday party." Yes: almost one-fourth (23 percent) of respondents.
- "I have had too much to drink at a work holiday party." Yes: one in five (20 percent).
- "I know someone who has been fired from a job for their behavior at a holiday party." Yes: one in seven (14 percent).

Some holiday party stories are pretty funny, like the old joke about the tipsy guy with the lampshade on his head, but now smartphones are everywhere. If someone who's a little toasted says or does something stupid, it's no surprise to find it on social media the next day.

You have a duty to your people to prevent them from being overserved. One solution is to contract out to a licensed caterer. At a small party, you might issue each person two drink coupons at entry. Of course, having the party at a restaurant may be simpler. In any case, be sure there are plenty of nonalcoholic beverage choices.

Here are some ideas for making your party fun and successful:

- Be sure the invitation is clear about the time — starting and ending — and location. Bear in mind that it will be dark early. Also, parking may be an issue to address.

- Specify who's invited (typically, employee and spouse or guest), and mention appropriate apparel.

- Have an agreement on whether to "talk shop" or not.

- If you want to do a gift exchange, here's the quick and simple way: everybody brings a wrapped $10 gift and puts it on the entry table. Each person chooses one to take on the way out. Longer alternative: give out the gifts at the party. Everyone opens them on the spot. Fun for all! Google "gift exchange" for variations.

- Consider making a group donation of canned food or money to a charity.

- Take some notes about what worked and what could be better next year.

In December, most retail businesses are gearing up to take **year-end inventory**. Nobody wants to do all this on New Year's Day so some of it becomes a December priority. And remember, you need to prepare to **close out your books** and reset them on January 1.

Have a safe and fun December!

49 RETAIL SHRINKAGE AND LOSS PREVENTION

QUESTION:

I think my retail business might have a shrinkage problem. I don't want to think that my customers or employees are ripping me off. How can I get a handle on this?

ANSWER:

Yes, it's an ugly subject. And it certainly won't be made better by your head-in-the-sand approach. I can assure you that your business, and practically every other business, DOES have a theft problem. The question is, how big is it? And then, how can you effectively deal with it?

Let's talk about this.

First off, we need to define the problem. Shrinkage (or shrink) is commonly defined as the loss of inventory by stealing. For a retail store, one source of shrinkage is the theft of merchandise by customers, otherwise known as shoplifting. You also hear this called "boosting" or "five finger discount." This is commonly done by someone who appears to be a paying customer but actually conceals merchandise and takes it out of the store without paying for it. We'll talk about details in a moment.

The other component of shrinkage is employee theft. Again, this is very common in a retail business, where inventory is available in quantity — but it's also common in many other types of business. For example, an office employee might order a two-pack of printer cartridges and take one of them home for personal use. This is often called "backdoor theft," and you'd be surprised at how ingenious some of the methods can be.

You need to address this straight on. That means look in the mirror and realize that, yes, some of my employees are probably dishonest. It's an unpleasant thought, but as the old saying goes, locks are just there to keep honest people honest.

Here's the scope of this problem: according to the National Retail Federation (NRF, *nrf.com*), shrinkage cost retailers about $62 billion in 2019. And when we say, "cost retailers," that really means that the rest of us paid that $62 billion by paying more for the products that we bought. Ouch!

According to NRF Vice President of Loss Prevention Bob Moraca, "A common misperception about shoplifting is that retailers can afford the loss of a candy bar or a pair of jeans, but the truth is that the industry loses billions of dollars each year at the hands of callous criminals that could be put towards human capital, promotions, and other necessary business operations."

Richard Hollinger, a criminologist at the University of Florida, oversees the NRF survey. He notes that the loss has decreased recently, and that's a good thing, right? Well, yes and no. Hollinger attributes the decrease in loss to big retailers "implementing and updating loss prevention strategies in order to reduce shrinkage."

But here's the rub: all the retailers in the survey are very large retail chains. They are investing heavily in loss-prevention (LP) measures like real-time monitored cameras, hi-tech price tags, and well-trained specialized security staff. This makes sense because big-box retail is very competitive. Even a fraction of a percent in profit margin is big money.

That's fine for the big guys, but for small retailers, those LP measures aren't practical. The obvious conclusion is that the shoplifters will increasingly move to target smaller businesses which don't have those strong LP measures in place.

Here are three classic shoplifting examples:

- Several people come in and look around. Pretty soon, there's a phony slip-and-fall accident. While everyone rushes to aid the perceived victim, his or her colleagues pocket the targeted merchandise.

- Two people begin arguing loudly in a corner of your store. The other customers and staff are all distracted. Meanwhile, an accomplice loads up and leaves.

- An attractive young couple shows up with a small baby in a carriage. The carriage actually has a large empty compartment in the bottom. While the mother seems to have trouble maneuvering the vehicle around, the dad is "helpfully" leaning down and packing items into the compartment.

Note that these are really just different forms of creating a diversion that seems legitimate at the time. For a real eye-opener, Google "shoplifting techniques." Be prepared for some coarse language because many of the sites are actually instructions on how to shoplift.

And here's another oldie: our busy holiday season is in winter. Unless you plan on opening your next store in Australia, you have to expect that most every holiday customer will have on heavy outerwear. Wearing a large and bulky coat with a hidden slit in the bottom of an outside pocket, a booster can readily pocket items with minimal risk of detection.

50 MY BUSINESS IS IN TROUBLE …

QUESTION:
I can't admit this to anyone but I'm afraid my small business is in trouble and may even be in danger of going under. What can I do?

ANSWER:
Well, that's a dark thought. Good for you for facing up to it. And it's no comfort for you to see that some other small business owners may be in the same boat. You need to know more about the situation and your options.

Let's talk about this.

First off, you may think this is a big secret, but it's not. Most everybody you deal with — vendors, employees, probably even your customers or clients — already know what's going on.

To be blunt, here are the stakes. If you can take prompt and direct action, you may pull your business out of the skid. But if you wait, things will likely get worse.

Now is the time to get some outside advice. Pull together whatever financial statements you have and seek counsel. Here are some options: find a mentor or other trusted person to talk with. Call and get an appointment with SCORE. Set up meetings with your advisory board (accountant, banker, attorney, others). If your business is very small and you don't have an attorney on your team, realize that many local professionals, especially at smaller firms, will have an initial meeting with you at a reduced fee.

Two immediate and fatal danger signals are (1) continuously declining sales and (2) falling behind in paying quarterly payroll taxes or collected sales tax. These are the start of what's called the "death spiral," where the worse it gets, the worse it gets.

First thing to do immediately is cut expenses. This will be ugly. Realize that if you delay, it will be uglier. This could mean layoffs, benefit cuts, postponed maintenance, dumping nonessentials, even downsizing to a cheaper location.

You probably can't market your way out of the hole. Consider this: if you spend $1,000 on advertising, you may or may not get back much of the $1,000. But if you cut $1,000 worth of expenses, you save the full $1,000 right now. The exception to this is a very high-margin service business — for example, a hair salon or a professional service — where only your time is involved.

Although shutting down your business is the last resort, it may make sense. However, recognize that there are several things you can do before that drastic move. Some examples and strategies:

- Make a list of your business's strengths, and then be frank about your business's weak spots. Share this with your advisory board for their thoughts.
- Ask any customers who owe you money to pay it promptly.
- Ask vendors and trade creditors to take a discount on what you owe them.
- If you rent space, ask your landlord for a rent deferral.
- If you have excess or old inventory, mark it down and get rid of it.
- Consider retargeting your business to a different market. For example, an upscale retailer may be able to remarket itself to a more mid-market clientele.
- Consider trying to sell your business as a going concern. If there's a valid business structure left, that's possible. But realize that it's very unlikely anyone would buy a hurting business at more than a very distressed price.

- Be sure your business fully uses free internet and social media marketing opportunities.

- Can you resuscitate the business with cash from another source, like friends or family?

- Danger! Be very careful about putting up your personal home equity as collateral for what is in reality a pretty risky business loan.

Also, there is a fallback position short of closing down entirely. You could "hibernate" the business, keeping your options open for a later time. This means you would shut down and store the physical assets (for example, inventory and equipment) to bring back at a later time. Remember to put your business licenses and permits on "inactive" status.

And last, two outreach issues. If you have any secured creditors (lenders who can grab your business assets), talk with them. If you have thoughts of filing bankruptcy, get legal help immediately.

Bravo to you for facing this problem now, while you can still do something about it, and best wishes.

APPENDIX I:
I HEAR A LOT OF BUSINESS JARGON.

CAN WE HAVE SOME FUN WITH THIS?

QUESTION:
I'm pretty new to business and it seems like there are lots of words and phrases I don't get. What are some examples of unusual business sayings and terms?

ANSWER:
The business world has a second language, loaded with technospeak and accounting terms. There also is a third layer with thousands of creative and interesting "insider" business terms that may be new to you.

Let's have a little fun and talk about this.

Here are some examples from this parallel vocabulary of amusing business terms and phrases. While some are light and humorous, many are critical. Some are new and some have been around a while. Suggestion: mention a few at a staff meeting and have people guess and discuss what they mean. Here we go:

Chair plug. A person who attends meetings but seldom contributes any comments or ideas of value.

In a gadget trance. Someone just got a new tech device and can't take their eyes or hands off it.

Big hat, no cattle. Refers to someone who talks a good line but doesn't have much money or produce many workable ideas.

Rank and yank. This is a management technique (from Jack Welch at GE) in which all employees are evaluated on performance, and the lowest-rated are fired. Also called "groom and broom."

Seagull manager. The term became popular through a joke in Ken Blanchard's book *Leadership and the One Minute Manager*: "Seagull managers fly in, make a lot of noise, dump on everyone, then fly out," leaving others to clean up the mess.

Greenwashing. This derogatory term merges the concepts of "green" (environmentally sound) and "whitewashing" (to gloss over wrongdoing).

Low-drag employee. A new hire with few ties: no spouse, no children, and mobile.

Blamestorming. Having a group discussion of why a deadline was missed or a project failed. It usually ends with identification and blaming of the responsible party or parties.

WOMBAT. This harsh evaluation is an acronym for "waste of money, brains, and talent."

Chipmunking. Picture someone in a meeting hunched over and madly texting on a smartphone or other device. Similar: thumb jockey.

Screwdriver shop. A dismissive term for a business or department that doesn't really add much value to its products — just assembles a few parts and sends them out.

Mind the KPIs. This refers to the company's key performance indicators. Examples include sales volume, client counts, or other important tracking data. These may also be called metrics.

I paid some tuition on that. A slang reference to how someone lost money on a deal but learned a valuable lesson that made it worthwhile.

Foamed the runway. This means that a dire situation was averted at the very last moment. For example, an investor came in with a cash infusion just before bankruptcy.

Burn rate. A startup business will eat into its initial capital until it becomes cash flow positive. The amount of cash consumed (usually monthly) is called the burn rate.

Deadfish, Idaho. This fictional town is used as a marketing destination: "That's a good ad campaign idea, but how will you sell it in Deadfish, Idaho?"

Click and mortar. A brick and mortar (physical) retail store with a very strong website presence.

Side hustle. A second source of income from additional work other than your main job.

Mouse milking. This term derides a task or project that is theoretically possible but would require a great deal of effort and likely not yield much in return.

Al desco. Describes any meal eaten at a desk.

Chartjunk. Excessive visual material — for example, in a PowerPoint slide — that doesn't add any information or value to the graphic.

From the helicopter view. Suggests a big-picture approach to the issue at hand.

Stress puppy. A coworker who thrives on being stressed out and whiny.

One-banana task. This refers to a problem or duty that's so simple a chimpanzee could take care of it. If slightly more difficult, it's a two-banana task.

Sticky bottom. This describes a company where it's difficult to advance above entry level.

Pity party. Also called a pink slip party, where recently or soon-to-be laid-off employees meet and commiserate about their situation.

These phrases might give you a feel for how creative people in the business world deal with their situations and coworkers. For hundreds more, Google "business jargon" and see what looks interesting.

APPENDIX II:
RESOURCES

Websites:

aarp.org/work/small-business

americassbdc.org

annualcreditreport.com

avery.com

bbb.org

biznamewiz.com

bloomberg.com/businessweek

bplans.com/sample-business-plans

businessballs.com

businesscards24.com

businessknowhow.com

carolroth.com

cdc.gov

constantcontact.com

craigslist.org

delta7.com

ehow.com

entrepreneur.com

etsy.com

fastcap.com

forbes.com

franchise.org

franchiseregistry.com

ftc.gov

gotprint.com

greenbiz.com

irs.gov

karrass.com

khanacademy.org

knowthis.com

lean.org

lendingclub.com

marketresearch.com

martinlindstrom.com

mindtools.com

moo.com

mybusiness.com.au

myfico.com

naics.com

namefind.com

negotiationtraining.com.au/articles

nfib.com

nolo.com

nrf.com

paloalto.com

panabee.com

prosper.com

rocketlawyer.com

sba.gov

score.org

smallbiztrends.com

theGlobe.com

trademarkia.com

tsnn.com

unhappyfranchisee.com

uspto.gov

vistaprint.com

wikihow.com/write-a-press-release

Software:

QuickBooks

Organizations:

AARP
Chamber of Commerce (local)
Department of Revenue
Dow Jones Sustainability Index (DJSI)
Economic Development Department (local)
Equifax
Experian
Federal Trade Commission
International Franchise Association
IRS (local)
North American Industry Classification System (NAICS)
National Research Program
Risk Management Association
Secretary of State (local)
Small Business Administration
Small Business Development Center (local)
Toastmasters
Trade assocations
TransUnion

Books:

Bluman, Allan. *Business Math Demystified*. McGraw Hill. 2006

Chiaravalle, Bill and Barbara Findlay Schenck. *Branding For Dummies*. For Dummies. 2014

Gage, David. *The Partnership Charter*. Basic Books. 2004.

Kamoroff, Bernard. *Small Time Operator: How to Start Your Own Business, Keep Your Books, Pay Your Taxes, and Stay Out of Trouble*. Lyons Press. 2019.

Kraynak, Cecie. *Starting a Business All-In-One For Dummies*. For Dummies. 2015

Lakein, Alan. *How to Get Control of Your Time and Your Life*. Signet. 1989.

Levinson, Jay Conrad. *Guerrilla Marketing: Secrets for Making Big Profits from Your Small Business*. Houghton Mifflin. 1983.

Lindstrom, Martin. *Buyology: Truth and Lies About Why We Buy*. Broadway Books, 2010.

Packard, Vance. *The Hidden Persuaders*. lg Publishing 2007.

Putnam, Cara C, J.D. *The Complete Idiot's Guide to Business Law*. Alpha. 2009

SCORE Association. *SCORE Marketing Cookbook*. SCORE Association. 2012.

Strauss, Steven. *The Small Business Bible: Everything You Need to Know to Succeed in Your Small Business*. Wiley. 2012.

Tarcy, Brian and Hap Klopp. *The Complete Idiot's Guide to Business Management*. Alpha. 1997

Thiel, Peter. *Zero to One: Notes on Startups, or How to Build the Future*. Random House. 2014.

Underhill, Paco. *Why We Buy: The Science Of Shopping*. Simon & Schuster 2020.

People:

Bob Moraca
Dave Ramsey
Eric Ries
James Womack
Jay Arthur
Jeffrey Liker
Mark Graban
Mark Zuckerberg
Peter F. Drucker
Richard Hollinger
Salman Khan

Articles/Videos:

"90% of Companies Will Throw Holiday Parties This Year" (Battalia Winston Survey)

theatlantic.com/national/archive/2012/11/90-companies-will-throw-holiday-parties-year/320958/

"Why Millennials Want To Be Leaders In The Workplace Now More Than Ever" (*Forbes*)

forbes.com/sites/sarahlandrum/2017/12/01/why-millennials-want-to-be-leaders-in-the-workplace-now-more-than-ever/?sh=518c9a5e355d

"You Are Not Special (YouTube video)
youtube.com/watch?v=_lfxYhtf8o4

www.ingramcontent.com/pod-product-compliance
Lightning Source LLC
Chambersburg PA
CBHW040854210326
41597CB00029B/4848